MAKING SENSE
IN PSYCHOLOGY
AND THE
LIFE SCIENCES

a student's guide
to writing and style

Margot Northey & Brian Timney

Toronto
Oxford University Press

1986

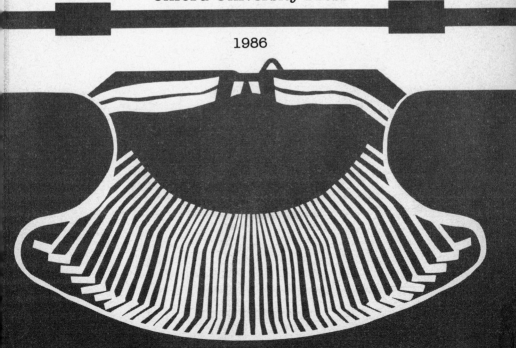

Canadian Cataloguing in Publication Data

Making sense in psychology and the life sciences

Includes index.

ISBN 0-19-540543-9

1. Exposition (Rhetoric).   2. Psychology - Authorship.   3. Life sciences -
Authorship.   4. Report writing.   5. English language - Rhetoric.
I. Timney, Brian.   II. Title.

BF76.7N.67 1986   808'.06615021   C86-093840-9

Cover illustration by Victoria Birta

2 3 4 - 9 8 7
Printed in Canada by Webcom Limited

Contents

Acknowledgements

A number of people at the University of Western Ontario helped in the preparation of this revised edition of *Making Sense* by providing information, suggesting material to be included, and making critical comments on the manuscript. In particular, we would like to thank Don Desserud of the Sciences Library for his help with the chapter on obtaining information and doing library research. Richard Zajchowski, a study-skills counsellor, kindly allowed us to use some of his ideas on preparing for multiple-choice exams. The section on studying for exams is based on suggestions in "Developing Your Study Skills," prepared by Bonnie Reberg, Fiona Goodchild, Joan Fleet, and Louise Tamblyn for the Counselling and Career Development Centre at Western, and is presented with their permission. We are also grateful to Vanessa Russell and Cathy Bryans, who assisted by checking out references and proofreading several versions of the text. Finally, we would like to thank Sally Livingston and Richard Teleky, our editors at Oxford University Press, for making the preparation of this book a pleasurable experience.

Symbols for common errors

NOTE: If any of the following markings appears on one of your essays
or reports, consult Chapter 9 or 10, or the Glossary, for help.

agr	agreement of subject and verb
amb	ambiguity
awk	awkwardness
cap	capitalization
cs	comma splice
D	diction
dang	dangling modifier (*or* dm)
frag	sentence fragment
gr	grammar or usage
mod	misplaced modifier
¶	new paragraph
//	parallelism
P	punctuation
quot	quotation marks
ref	pronoun reference
rep	repetition
RO	run-on sentence
sp	spelling
SS	sentence structure
sp inf	split infinitive
sub	subordination
T	tense
trans	transition
⌒	transpose (change order of letters or words)
wdy	wordy
ww	wrong word

A note to the student

Contrary to many students' belief, good writing does not come naturally; even for the best writers it's mostly hard work, following the old formula of ten per cent inspiration and ninety per cent perspiration.

Writing in university or college is not fundamentally different from writing anywhere else. Yet each piece of writing has its own special purposes, and these are what determine its particular substance, shape, and tone. In this book we will examine both the general precepts for effective writing and the special requirements of scientific writing (especially the lab report and the research paper); we will also point out some of the most common errors in student composition and suggest how to avoid or correct them. Written mostly in the form of guidelines rather than strict rules — since few rules are inviolable — *Making Sense in Psychology and the Life Sciences* should help you escape the common pitfalls of student writing and develop confidence through an understanding of basic principles and a mastery of sound techniques.

1
Writing and thinking in the sciences

No matter whether you are writing an essay in history or a review paper in microbiology, you are not likely to produce clear writing unless you have first done some clear thinking, and thinking can't be hurried. It follows that one of the most important things you can do is to leave yourself enough time to think.

Several studies have shown that we don't always solve a difficult problem by "putting our mind to it." Sometimes when we are stuck it's best to take a break and let our creativity work subconsciously for a while. Very often a period of relaxation will produce a new approach or solution. Just remember that leaving time for creative reflection isn't the same thing as sitting around listening to the stereo until inspiration strikes out of the blue.

Knowing what you want to say is only the first step, though. Much of the time you will be trying to convey complicated factual information. Your main task is to convince the person who reads your paper that you know what you are talking about. You can only do this if the reader can easily understand what you have written. Therefore you must think not only about what you want to say, but about how you are going to say it.

INITIAL STRATEGIES

To write is to make choices. Certainly practice makes the decisions easier to come by, but no matter how fluent you become, with each piece of writing you will still have to choose. You can narrow the field of choice from the start if you realize that you are *not* writing for anybody, anywhere, for no particular reason. In university (or anywhere else), it is always sound strategy to ask yourself two basic questions:

- What is the purpose of this piece of writing?
- What is the reader like?

Although your first reaction may be "Well, I'm writing to satisfy a course requirement for my professor," that is not going to get you very far.

Think about the purpose

Your purpose may be any of several possibilities:

- to describe and interpret an experiment you have done;
- to show that you understand certain terms or theories;
- to show that you can do independent library research;
- to provide information about a topic;
- to show your knowledge of a topic;
- to show that you can think clearly and critically.

If you are reviewing a body of literature, the way you construct your paper will be different from what it would be if you were discussing the merits of two opposing theories. If you don't have the exact purpose clear in your own mind, you may find yourself working at cross purposes — and wasting a lot of time.

Think about the reader

Thinking about the reader does *not* mean playing up to the teacher. To convince a particular person that your own views are sound and that you know what you are talking about, you have to consider the intellectual context in which he or she operates. If you were to write a paper for a biology course on the effects of certain drugs it would be quite different from one on the same topic submitted for a psychology course. You have to make specific decisions about the background information you will supply, the terms you will need to explain, and the amount of detail that is appropriate. When you are writing a lab report, you need to give much more procedural detail than you would if you were writing a review of the same topic. If you don't know who will be reading your paper—your professor, your tutorial leader, or a marker—just imagine someone intelligent, well-informed and interested, skeptical enough to question your ideas but flexible enough to accept them if your evidence is convincing.

You must remember also that the person who reads your paper can only read what is on the page, not what is in your head. This is especially true when you are writing lab reports. Don't take it for granted that your reader has detailed knowledge about your experimental procedure, for example. Your work will be judged in part on how well you can describe what you have done.

Think about the length

Before you start writing, you will also need to think about the length of the assignment in relation to the time you have available to spend on it. If both the topic and the length are prescribed, it should be fairly easy for you to assess the level of detail required and the amount of research you need to do. If only the length is prescribed, that restriction will help you decide how broad or how narrow a topic you should choose.

Think about the tone

In everyday writing to friends you probably take a casual tone, but academic writing is usually more formal. The exact degree of formality will depend on the kind of assignment and instructions you have been given. In some cases—say, if your psychology professor asks you to keep a journal describing certain personal experiences—you may well be able to use an informal style. Lab reports and review papers, however, require a more formal tone. This is particularly important in scientific writing, when you need to express yourself unambiguously. On the other hand, you should also avoid the other extreme of excessive formality.

What kind of style is inappropriate for most scientific writing? Here are the main signs:

Use of slang

A slang word or phrase is hardly ever appropriate in a science paper. If you described a rat moving quickly down one arm of a maze as "going like a bat out of hell," you might convey the wrong impression. Another reason for not using slang expressions is that they are often regional and short-lived: they may mean different things to different groups at different times. (Think of how the meaning of the terms *hot* and *cool* can vary, depending on the circumstances.)

Frequent use of contractions

Generally speaking, contractions such as *can't* and *isn't* are not suitable for scientific writing, although they may be fine for letters or other informal kinds of writing—for example, this handbook.

Excessive use of first-person pronouns

If you are writing a lab report about an experiment you have done, there is no need to keep reminding the reader of your involvement. However, occasional use of first-person pronouns is quite acceptable if the choice is between using *I* or *we* and creating a tangle of passive constructions. (A hint: when you do use *I*, it will be less noticeable if you place it in the middle of the sentence rather than at the beginning.)

2
Obtaining
information

One of the most important rules about writing a scientific paper is that what you say must be supported by evidence. This rule applies no matter what you're writing—a lab report for a classroom project or a review paper for publication in a professional journal. If you are going to make a career as a scientist, you will quickly find out that you must be able to support your arguments with facts. For this reason it is important that you learn how to track down information very early in your career. At present your most pressing need will be to find the references that will help you to complete your assignments, but once you know how to obtain information, you will have a powerful academic tool to work with.

If you are just starting your university career, your assignments will probably not require extensive library research. All the same, if you train yourself to find information efficiently, the skill will be useful to you in many different situations.

WHERE TO START

Since the guidelines in this chapter apply to any kind of scientific research, let's assume that your topic has already been determined. (For details on planning a proper research paper, see Chapter 6.) Your first task is to find out who and what the major authors and references are in that particular field. With this information you can begin to look more systematically for relevant papers. If you have absolutely no knowledge about your topic, take the shotgun approach: look everywhere, but do it superficially. Here are two of the best ways to get at least a general idea of what is going on in an area:

Ask other people

It's surprising, but not many students take advantage of their primary resource-person: their course instructor. Although you should not expect to be provided with all the information you will need, your instructor should be able to give you some names and references to get you started. Similarly, if you have a graduate teaching assistant, or even friends you know to be more knowledgeable than you about a particular topic, don't be afraid to ask.

Browse around the library

An efficient strategy for getting a sense of what is going on in a field is to browse through some of the primary and secondary sources. For example, let's say that you want to write an essay on congenital insensitivity to pain. You know that the literature on pain is vast, and you also know that there is relatively little information on congenital insensitivity. You might adopt the following procedure:

1. Look at the subject-heading index in your library's cataloguing system. You might start with "pain" as a general heading, or you might try to narrow down your search by looking at terms such as "pain–insensitivity" or "hypoalgesia" or "analgesia." A quick glance through the catalogue will show you that most of the books on pain have similar call numbers.
2. Once you find the appropriate stack, browse through some of the textbooks that are there. You don't have to look for specific works: just go through the indexes of different texts for any reference to pain insensitivity. Even if you don't find a full book on the subject you're interested in, you should find a few relevant references and begin to see how the topic has been discussed by different people.
3. Another place to look is in the journals specializing in your topic. Much of the research on pain, for instance, is published in the journal *Pain*. If you go to the current-periodicals section of your library and skim through the Contents pages of all *Pain* issues for the past year or so, you might find something useful. This technique doesn't always work, but if it does it can give you a lot of information. Not only will you have an up-to-date article on your topic, but if you look at the reference list at the end of it you should find a number of other recent references.

SYSTEMATIC MANUAL SEARCHES

The strategies outlined above will help you get some start-up information, but if you are writing a review of a body of literature you will need a much more extensive list of references. You can do this in two ways: manually, as described below, or by using an on-line data base, described in the next section.

Using secondary sources

If someone has written a review paper on your topic in the last few years and it includes a listing of relevant earlier literature, you can then concentrate on tracking down more recent references. In many cases your textbook will refer to review papers; otherwise your professor may be able to suggest one. If not, you may still be able to get some leads in the library.

One of the best sources is the *Index of Scientific Reviews*. This is a serial publication listing review articles and chapters that have appeared in the recent scientific literature. The fact that sources are filed under different subject headings and are extensively cross-referenced means that you have a number of possibilities to look under if you aren't sure of the best way to describe what you want.

Another useful source is the Annual Review series. These books, made up of review chapters, are published each year and provide detailed summaries of current research. The series includes, among many others, these: the *Annual Review of Psychology*, the *Annual Review of Neuroscience*, the *Annual Review of Physiology*, the *Annual Review of Genetics*, and the *Annual Review of Entomology*. These works are particularly helpful because they cover most of the sub-areas of each discipline and commission new reviews on the same topics every few years.

Using the abstract and index journals

If you are forced to look for all your references from scratch, one of the most thorough (though not the most efficient) approaches is to use the abstract or index journals. You will find a surprising number of such journals in the reference section of your library. Covering almost every major subdivision of the life sciences, they range from *Aquatic Sciences and Fisheries Abstracts* to *Weed Abstracts*. Among the most useful are *Biological Abstracts, Excerpta Medica, Index Medicus,* and *Psychological Abstracts.*

Abstract journals contain numbered listings of abstracts of publications organized under a wide variety of subheadings. If you know the heading your topic of interest is likely to fall under, simply look it up in the subject index to obtain the numbers of the abstracts dealing with it. Then look through each of the abstracts to see if the material is relevant to your needs. You can do the same thing with an index journal, such as *Index Medicus,* except that it lists only the title of the publication, without an abstract.

Although you can obtain a tremendous amount of information by searching the abstracts and indexes, the procedure can be time-consuming and frustrating. In order to get a few references on your topic you may have to look through a large number of abstracts containing irrelevant information—you can spend an afternoon at the library and not have much to show for it. On the positive side, an abstract search will often turn up papers that you might not have found otherwise. Also, you may find that after browsing through the abstracts you have become familiar with some of the important names in the field and the kinds of experiments that are being done.

Science Citation Index (SCI)

Another kind of index that allows you to find references, though in a somewhat different way, is the *Science Citation Index (SCI).* While the abstracts and indexes may be thought of as subject-oriented sources, *SCI* allows you to track down references through authors. It also allows you to search forward in time; that is, if you know of an important paper written by a certain author several years ago, you can find out who has referred to that paper subsequently.

There are several different sections of *SCI,* but the most important part for you will be the *Citation Index* itself. The best way to show you how to use it is to give you an example.

Imagine that you want to find more about the effects of a person's being born blind and later having his or her sight restored; you also know of a relevant article by Brian Timney, published in the journal *Experimental Brain Research* in 1978. If you look up this reference in the *Citation Index* for 1984 you will see the entry as shown in part A of Figure 2.1. Your target is the author's name (1) with the abbreviated reference below it, both in boldface type. Below the reference are listed two articles—(2) and (3)—that cited the Timney paper in that year. These citations, taken from the list of references at the end of each of these articles, suggest that the authors may be discussing something that is relevant to your topic.

Figure 2.1 Part A

Citation Index

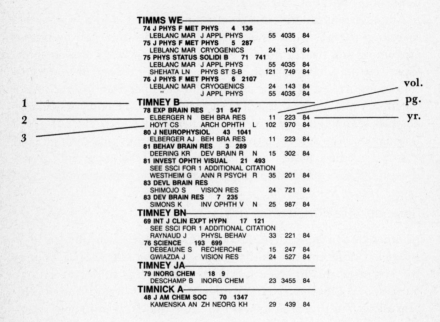

This is not always the case, however, and the *Citation Index* gives only the reference, not the title, of each article. To save time looking for these papers in the library stacks, you can go to the *Source Index* of *SCI*, as shown in part B. This gives the title of every paper referenced in the *Citation Index*, listed under authors. From there you can look up the papers that seem most useful to you. As you can see, the Elberger paper (4) is probably not pertinent, since it is about the *corpus callosum*. But the paper by Hoyt (5) does seem relevant, because it is concerned with the effects of visual deprivation in newborns. By

Figure 2.1 Part B

Source Index

ELBERD M
see ALLARDLA. G   ARCH MAL C   77   1403   84
ELBERG S
see BRAJTBUR. J   ANTIM AG CH   26   892   84
see   "   CLIN RES   32   A557   84
see   "   J INFEC DIS   149   986   84
ELBERGER AJ
• THE EXISTENCE OF A SEPARATE, BRIEF CRITICAL PERIOD
FOR THE CORPUS-CALLOSUM TO AFFECT VISUAL
DEVELOPMENT
BEH BRA RES   11(3):223-231   84   52R
UNIV TEXAS SCH MED DEPT NEUROBIOL & ANAT. HOUSTON,
TX   77025 USA
• THE MINIMUM EXTENT OF CORPUS-CALLOSUM
CONNECTIONS REQUIRED FOR NORMAL VISUAL
DEVELOPMENT IN THE CAT
HUM NEUROB   3(2):115-120   84   37R
UNIV TEXAS, SCH MED, DEPT NEUROBIOL & ANAT, HOUSTON,
TX   77025 USA
ELBERLING C
• DON M — QUALITY ESTIMATION OF AVERAGED AUDITORY
BRAIN-STEM RESPONSES
SC AUDIOL   13(3):187-197   84   11R
HOUSE EAR INST, ELECTROPHYSIOL LAB, LOS ANGELES, CA
ELBERLING JA
see NAGASAWA HT   J MED CHEM   27   1335   84

4

HOYT AM
see WHITAKER JE   J PHARM SCI   73   1184   84
HOYT BK
• WOLF HK — AN ELECTRONIC INSTRUMENT FOR INDIRECT
BLOOD-PRESSURE MEASUREMENT ▶ NOTE
LANCET   2(8402):552-553   84   4R
DALHOUSIE UNIV. DEPT PHYSIOL & BIOPHYS. HALIFAX
B3H 4H7, NS, CANADA
HOYT CS
• JASTRZEB GB MARG E — AMBLYOPIA AND CONGENITAL
ESOTROPIA — VISUALLY EVOKED-POTENTIAL MEASUREMENTS
ARCH OPHTH   102(1):58-61   84   28R
UNIV CALIF, SAN FRANCISCO, SCH MED DEPT OPHTHALMOL.
SAN FRANCISCO, CA 94143, USA
• ANOTHER LOOK AT LONG-TERM VISUAL EFFECTS OF
BINOCULAR OCCLUSION IN NEONATES — REPLY ▶ LETTER
ARCH OPHTH   102(7):970   84   2R
see BALKMAN R   AM J OPHTH   97   315   84
see FARMER J   "   98   504   84
see JASTRZEB GB   ARCH OPHTH   102   1030   84
see SKARF B   "   102   62   84
HOYT D
see CURTIS LR   J PHARM EXP   231   495   84
HOYT DB
• GREENBURAG FORBES S LIN S — FLUOROCARBON
RESUSCITATION IN HEMORRHAGIC SHOCK ▶ MEETING
J TRAUMA   24(7):663   84   NO   R
VET ADM MED CTR. DEPT SURG. SAN DIEGO, CA 92161
see LEE E   J TRAUMA   24   667   84

5

looking at the references in the Hoyt paper, you may find additional
studies useful to you. If you use *SCI* thoughtfully you can build up a
collection of core references that will allow you to make progressively
wider searches. If you are preparing the introduction to a thesis you
may need to search much more widely, but for a short class essay you
may be able to stop your search once you have tracked down the major
papers in an area.

ON-LINE DATA BASES

Over the past few years many of the abstract and index journals, including *Science Citation Index*, *Index Medicus*, and *Psychological Abstracts*, have been stored as computer files accessible through your library's computer or, if you wish, through your own personal computer. Hundreds of data bases are now available, covering every conceivable topic. Your library will probably have access to several of these, depending on which services it subscribes to. Although these services are used mostly by graduate students and faculty members, there is no reason not to use them for an undergraduate paper. For a short essay, obviously, you do not need to go to such lengths, but for major research papers an on-line search is well worth considering (it is usually not very expensive).

Why use an on-line data base?

You can gather a tremendous amount of information from the abstract journals and *Science Citation Index*, but the job can be slow and painful. It would be much quicker if you had someone else to do the searching for you. In a way, this is what you get with an on-line data base. There are three advantages to using such a system:

- speed of access;
- comprehensiveness of the search;
- access to unlikely sources or to those that are not readily available.

With such vast amounts of information available, your problem becomes one of restricting it to manageable levels. A careless search can turn up hundreds of articles, most of which are completely irrelevant, but if the job is done properly you may find most of the references you need in a very short time.

Rules for good on-line searches

It may be possible to do a search yourself, but you will usually be much better off if you allow a librarian to do the searching on the basis of information you provide. (In most libraries this is the only way to get a search done.) By far the most satisfactory arrangement is one in which you can discuss your needs with the searcher, who will then set up the most efficient search strategy. However, you can assist the search process greatly if you know a little about the logic underlying on-line searches.

Although the various data bases function somewhat differently, all require that you enter certain relevant keywords that the computer can search for. These may be contained in the title or the abstract of the paper, or they may be part of a list of *descriptors* assigned to the paper by an indexer. When you do a search you should use enough keywords to be sure that you do not miss large numbers of references, but not so many that you come up with a great deal of irrelevant material.

The most efficient way to use keywords is to follow the rules of Boolean logic, which allow you to combine search terms using the logical operators *and*, *not*, and *or*. For example, suppose you have been assigned a biology paper on the feeding habits of blowflies. You might begin a general search using the terms *Blowfly or Phormia regina* and *Feeding or Hunger or Eating*. This will get you a list of papers whose titles or descriptors contained a reference to blowflies in conjunction with feeding, hunger, or eating. If this initial search produces too many references for your purposes, or if many of them are not closely related to what you are looking for, you can narrow the search by including more keywords such as *behaviour*, *taste*, or *preference*. By selecting the appropriate combination of terms a skilled searcher can usually come up with a moderate list of references, most of which will be of some use to you. Once you have these references, you can track down more using the references given in each article.

TAKING GOOD NOTES

Finding your research material is one thing; taking notes that are dependable and easy to use is another. With time you will develop your own best method, but to start you might try the index-card system. Record each reference on a separate index-card. Make sure you have the complete reference written down accurately, including page numbers. If it is a book, remember to put down the publisher and the place and date of publication. Be sure you also record the library call-number, in case you want to find the reference again. Nothing is more frustrating than discovering that you aren't sure where a piece of information came from when you want to cite it.

Below the reference, note the major points of the article. You don't need to go into much detail — just enough to help you remember what it was about. You can always go back if you need more information. It's also worthwhile to make a comment to remind yourself how you felt about the material. When you are doing your final write-up and see a reference noted "useful review," you might want to go back and read it over; if you see that another paper was "incomprehensible, too theoretical," you might decide to skip it.

3
Writing a lab report I: organization and format

If you are studying psychology or one of the biological sciences, such as microbiology or genetics, much of the written work you do as an undergraduate will be in the form of lab reports. Beyond the undergraduate level, the bulk of your scientific writing will be formal descriptions of experiments you have done.

Writing a lab report is a little different from writing an English essay. Although any kind of academic writing should be clear, concise, and forceful, there is one more imperative for scientific writing: be objective. Scientists are interested in the orderly presentation of factual evidence to support hypotheses or theories; therefore you must never allow your personal biases or expectations to get in the way of facts. You must present your information in such a way that anyone who reads your report can understand clearly what you've done in your experiment. On the basis of the evidence you present, readers should be free to draw their own conclusions. If you have done a good job, their conclusions will be the same as yours.

WRITING GUIDELINES

Formal style requirements vary quite widely, but the basic format of lab reports is generally similar. Although your lab instructor will give you the specific information for your discipline, for more detailed information on both style and format you might also consult the *Publication Manual of the American Psychological Association* (American Psychological Association, 1983) or the *CBE Style Manual* (Council of Biology Editors, 1983).

Over the past fifty years or so, the American Psychological Association (APA) has made available a set of guidelines for the preparation of manuscripts for publication. The most recent version of these guidelines is the third edition of their publication manual. Although it is directed mainly to those who publish in journals sponsored by the Association, its rules about format and style have been adopted by several disciplines as a guide for publishing and for writing lab reports. In this chapter we will present some of the APA rules of format and organization. The *CBE Style Manual* is most useful for those working in disciplines where it is important to be accurate when describing different species of plants or animals or different chemical compounds.

PURPOSE AND READER

The purpose of most of your undergraduate lab reports will be to show that you understand a phenomenon or theory, or that you know how to test a certain hypothesis. As is the case in professional scientific writing, you can assume that the reader — your instructor — is familiar with basic scientific terms, so you will not need to define or explain them. You can also assume that he or she will be on the lookout for any weaknesses in methodology or analysis and any omissions of important data. However, you cannot assume that your instructor is omniscient. It is very frustrating to read, for example, that "the subjects' settings were read directly from the micrometer drive," when this is the first time a micrometer has been mentioned anywhere in the paper. Be sure that you have mentioned pieces of equipment or procedures before you start making casual references to them.

Make an attractive presentation

Unfair as it may seem, whoever reads your report will be influenced by the look of the presentation — its physical appearance. Impressions count. Even if you have carried out the experiment perfectly and included all the appropriate information, if your write-up is a mess you probably won't receive as high a mark as the work deserves.

FORMAT

To make it easy for the reader to find and assess, the information in a scientific report should be organized into separate sections, each with a heading. By convention, most lab reports follow a standard order:

1. Title page
2. Abstract
3. Introduction
4. Method (may include some or all of the following subsections: Subjects, Design, Materials, Apparatus, Procedure)
5. Results
6. Discussion
7. References
8. Footnotes

The order of these sections is always the same, although some may be combined or have slightly different names, depending on the kind and amount of information you have in each one. (Different disciplines also have slightly different rules.) You can often make your paper clearer by including subheadings within each of these main sections.

Use of headings

The APA style permits up to five levels of headings:

LEVEL ONE
(centred, upper-case)
Level Two
(centred, upper- and lower-case)
Level Three
(centred, upper- and lower-case, underlined)

Level Four
(flush left, upper- and lower-case, underlined)
    Level five.
(indented, lower-case after initial letter, underlined, ending with a period and leading directly into paragraph).

You will rarely need to use all these levels; in most cases two will be enough:

Method	(Level 2)
<u>Procedure</u>	(Level 4)

If you need a third, add level 5:

Method	(Level 2)
<u>Subjects</u>	(Level 4)
<u>Control group.</u>	(Level 5)

If you have a series of experiments to describe, you may need to rearrange the headings:

Experiment 1	(Level 2)
<u>Method</u>	(Level 3)
<u>Subjects</u>	(Level 4)
<u>Control group.</u>	(Level 5)

These examples may not fit every situation; the most important thing to remember is that your headings should follow a logical and consistent pattern.

Title page

The first page of your report is always the title page. It will include the title of the paper, your name, the names of the course and the instructor, and the date of submission. The title should be brief but informative, clearly indicating the topic and scope of your study: use words that you think would be useful if you were doing a literature search for studies on your topic. Avoid meaningless phrases such as "A Study of . . ." or "Observations on . . ."; simply state what it is that you are studying; for example: "The Effects of Gamma Rays on the Growth Rate of Man-in-the-Moon Marigolds."

Abstract or Summary

The Abstract or Summary appears on a separate page following the title page. It is a brief summary of the purpose of the experiment, as well as the method, results, and conclusions. For a simple experiment it may be only a few lines, but even for a complex one it should not be more than about two hundred words. It should also be able to stand alone; that is, someone should be able to read your abstract and know exactly what the experiment was about, what the results were, and how you interpreted them.

Introduction

The Introduction should give a fairly detailed statement of your purpose or objective. It should include a brief review of the pertinent literature and, if appropriate, discuss the theory underlying the experiment. If, as is often the case, the purpose is to test a hypothesis about a specific problem, you should state clearly the nature of both the problem and the hypothesis. Remember, though, that not all experiments make predictions. Sometimes you may be asking a question without making a prediction—if you were interested in the social development of young infants, for example, you might ask at what age the baby first smiled and how the frequency of social smiling changed with age. But even if you do not have a specific prediction, you should state your question clearly.

Method

The Method section is usually made up of several subsections: subjects (the organisms you were working with), experimental apparatus and materials, and procedure.

Subjects

In psychology, or in other disciplines in which live animals are used in the experiment, you need a section describing your experimental animal. If these animals happen to be human, you need to give information about them that will be relevant to the experiment. For example, if you were studying people's judgements on the meanings of certain kinds of words, you should mention whether or not all of your subjects were native English speakers. Typically, you would also give the average age of the group and their status ("university undergraduates" or "three-year-old children registered in a pre-school program"). Your rule about what information to include should be "Is it relevant to the purpose of the study?" When you use non-human subjects you should mention the species or strain and any special characteristics that they might possess.

Materials

Depending on the discipline and the kind of experiment you are doing, this section may be entitled either Materials or Apparatus. Ask your instructor for the rules that apply to your own experiment. In general, it should describe all the materials—for instance, chemicals or psychological test batteries—and any experimental apparatus you used, including all the essential components of any major pieces of equipment and how they were set up. If different arrangements of equipment were required, give a full list of the equipment in this section, and then in the Procedure section describe each separate arrangement before you describe the respective procedures. When the equipment is a standard, commercially available item, it is customary to give the manufacturer's name and the model number; for example, if your psychology experiment required you to present patterns on the face of an oscilloscope cathode-ray tube, you might say that they were "presented on a Tektronix 608 display monitor with a P31 phosphor," or whatever it was that you used.

Procedure

This section is a step-by-step description of how you carried out the experiment. If you did a number of tests, you should begin with a short summary statement listing them, so that the reader will be prepared for the series; then, to avoid confusion, describe the tests in the same order.

The Procedure section must be written with enough detail that others would have no difficulty in repeating the experiment in all its essentials. However, you should avoid any detail that is not directly relevant to the study. For instance, if you were measuring the effectiveness of different antibiotics on bacterial growth, you would have to describe the volume of the solution containing the bacteria, its temperature, the strength and amount of antibiotic given, and so on; you would not need to mention that the experiment was carried out on the fifth floor of the biology building.

If you followed instructions in a lab manual you may not need to copy them out word for word; simply refer to the instructions and give details of any differences in your experiment.

You should describe your experiments in the past tense. When you want to give instructions rather than a description of your method, use the imperative: for example, "Cut off 1 cm from the bottom of the stem."

Scientists who publish in professional journals are divided as to whether you should use the active or passive voice. Traditionally, most have preferred the passive voice ("The rat was placed in the starting-box of the maze," rather than "I placed the rat in the starting-box") because they believed that its impersonal quality helped to maintain the detached, impartial tone appropriate for a scientific report. Nevertheless, some scientists have begun using the active voice because it is clearer and less likely to lead to awkward, convoluted sentences. Find out if your department has any preferences. If not, make your own judgement based on how well the passage reads and how clear it is. (Remember, too, that if you were the only one doing the experiment you should use *I* rather than *we*.)

Results

When professional scientists come across a new paper, often they will only glance at the Introduction and Methods, and concentrate on the Results section, because they know this is where they will find the most important information. In a sense, all other sections are subordinate to the Results. The only way readers can decide if they agree with your interpretation as presented in the Discussion is if they can make their own evaluation of the data, and the only way they can do that is if the results are presented clearly and unambiguously. For this reason you should spend some time thinking about the best way to present your results; you have a lot of choices, and some are much better than others. See the next chapter for a detailed discussion of presenting data.

Discussion

This is the part of the lab report that allows you the greatest freedom, since your purpose is to examine and interpret the results and to comment on their significance. You want to show how the experiment produced its outcome, whether expected or unexpected, and to discuss those elements that influenced the results.

Before you begin your actual discussion you should give a brief overview of the major findings of your study; for example: "The results of the present study demonstrated that university students could remember the details of lectures much better if they spent fifteen minutes organizing and expanding their lecture notes at the end of each class." The rest of the discussion would deal with the reasons why this should be so.

To help you decide what to include in the Discussion section, you might try to answer the following questions:

- Do the results reflect the objectives of the experiment?
- Do your results agree with previous results as reported in the literature on the subject? If not, how can you account for the difference? What, if anything, may have gone wrong during your experiment, and why? What was the source of any error?
- Could the results have another explanation?
- Did the procedures you used help you to accomplish the purpose of the experiment? Does your experience in this experiment suggest a better approach for next time?

The order of topics in your Discussion should be the same as that in your Results. Discuss each of your findings in turn as you reported them in the previous section. If you have a result that you don't know how to explain, say so; never ignore an inconvenient finding in the hope that your instructor might not notice. A good Discussion section may not be able to tie up all the loose ends, but it must acknowledge that they are there.

You should always end with a statement of the conclusions that may be drawn from the results of the experiment. Sometimes the conclusions are put in a separate section, but typically they form the final paragraph at the end of the Discussion. In the example above you might end this way: "The findings of the present study suggest that if students were able to take a little extra time going over their notes at the end of each class, it is likely that they could improve their grades."

References

Each time you refer to a book or an article in the text of your report, you should indicate the reference at that point and then at the end of the paper make a list of all the sources you have cited. The precise form of the citations varies quite a lot between disciplines; for more detail, see Chapter 5.

Footnotes

You should use footnotes as little as possible. If they are unavoidable, indicate where each one should go in the text by placing a number as a superscript at the point of insertion. At the end of the paper, after the references, list the footnotes in order, numbering them to correspond with the numbers you have in the text.

REFERENCES

American Psychological Association. (1983). *Publication manual of the American Psychological Association* (3rd ed.). Washington, DC: Author.

Council of Biological Editors. (1983). *CBE style manual. A guide for authors, editors, and publishers in the biological sciences* (5th ed.). Bethesda, MD.: Author.

4
Writing a lab report II: presentation of data

As mentioned in the previous chapter, the Results section is the heart of an experimental paper. If you don't present your results clearly, the lab report isn't worth reading. Once you have gathered a set of data, you will find that there are many ways of reporting them. Do you present a figure or a table? If you choose to make a figure, should it be a histogram or a graph? If it is a graph, how will you arrange the axes? In time the decisions will become much easier, but to start with you have to know what the possibilities are.

ORGANIZING A RESULTS SECTION

There are two main aspects to a set of experimental data: the raw data themselves and the results of any analysis of them that you choose to do. A good Results section should contain both a summary of the data and a report of the analyses. It is not unusual to see the Results section of a psychology experiment begin something like this: "An analysis of variance was done on the data and there was a significant main effect for x." This is not very informative. As a general rule, you should lead your reader through the data, one level of analysis at a time. Deal with the main findings first and then go on to the secondary results. The following approach is a good one:

1. Present a summary of the main results

It will be obvious that for most of your experiments you will have too many raw data to simply report all of them. Instead, you should summarize the data in a figure or a table supplemented with a verbal description. There is no firm rule on which to choose for each particular occasion, but the adage that a picture is worth a thousand words certainly applies in the case of presenting any numerical data.

For example, suppose you are carrying out an experiment examining the phototactic behavior of two different species of insect; that is, their tendency to approach or to avoid a light. You test 150 animals of each species by putting each insect individually into a box with a light at one end. After one minute you note how far that insect is away from the light. After you have done this for every insect, you will have a record of the numbers found at each distance. One way of reporting these data is in the form of a table (Table 4.1).

Table 4.1

Preferred distance from light source for two species of insect.								
Distance from light (cm)	0-5	5-10	10-15	15-20	20-25	25-30	30-35	35-40
Species 1	3	14	13	19	23	20	26	32
Species 2	4	7	22	30	37	30	15	5

Note: The values in the table represent the numbers of insects found at each distance from the light source 1 minute after the light had been turned on.

If you examine these numbers you can see that there is a tendency for insects of Species 1 to accumulate at the end of the box away from the light, while those of Species 2 tend to bc found in the middle of the box. A data table of this sort is a perfectly acceptable way of presenting your results. But contrast this table with Figure 4.1, showing the same set of data. You can see at a glance that the two species are quite different in their preferences. The actual numbers at each distance don't really matter; the figure illustrates the *pattern* of results, which is what is important. For more detail on preparing tables and graphs, see pages 27-31.

Figure 4.1

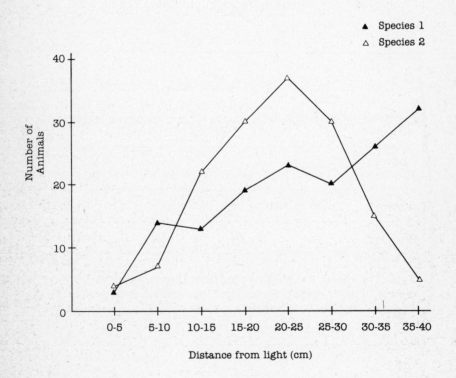

Distance from light (cm)

2. Include descriptive analyses and statistics

When you are measuring some characteristic of living organisms, there will almost always be variability over successive measurements. For this reason it is usual to make repeated measurements of the same thing and take an average. For instance, you might run a group of eight pigeons in a learning experiment to find out how many trials it takes them to learn a certain task. You may present the data from each animal if you wish, but you could provide more useful information by presenting a summary in the form of some descriptive statistics. In this example you might give the average number of trials taken by the birds in the group to learn the task, together with some estimate of the variability between different animals, such as the standard deviation. Summary statistics give your reader a lot of information in very few words.

3. Present your data analysis

In many experiments you are testing a hypothesis. Even if you are asking a question for which you do not have a specific prediction, your experiment may be set up formally as a test of a statistical hypothesis. For example, the question "What is the effect of different drugs on the rate at which rats learn to run through a maze without making errors?" might be rephrased as "Drug A produces significantly better learning than drug B." You could then test that hypothesis using the appropriate statistical tests. The results of any analysis you might do would then be presented after your descriptive statistics.

You should present first the actual statistical values and then a brief statement of what they mean. For example, if you had done the drugs-and-learning experiment you might have analysed your data using an analysis of variance. You could describe the results of your analysis this way: "The analysis of variance showed a significant difference in the effectiveness of the two drugs ($F(1,12) = 14.5$, $p < .01$); the rats that were given drug A took fewer trials to learn the task than those that received drug B." Again, the important thing to remember is to express yourself as clearly as possible.

Preparing tables

Your decision to make a table rather than a figure should be based on which will convey the information most effectively. In general, you would use a table for a set of several numbers that might not be clear if presented in the body of the text, but are not so complex that a figure is absolutely necessary. Consider the following: "After planting 100 seeds in each of fifteen boxes, five containing sandy soil, five containing rocky soil, and five clay, the average number of seedlings emerging from the different soil types was 20.2, 3.6, and 5.3 for Plant A in the sandy, rocky, and clay types respectively. It was 3.8, 0.2, and 30.7 for Plant B and 5.3, 7.4, and 3.0 for Plant C." Your readers will get a much better, clearer picture of what went on if you present these data in tabular form, as in Table 4.2.

Table 4.2

Average number of seedlings sprouting when planted in different soil types.

Average no. of seedlings sprouting	SOIL TYPE		
	Sandy	Rocky	Clay
Plant A	20.2	3.6	5.3
Plant B	3.8	1.2	30.7
Plant C	5.3	7.4	3.0

Note: The values represent the mean number of seedlings that sprouted out of each group of 100 planted. Five samples of each kind of plant were planted in each soil type.

If you do decide to make a table, ask yourself these questions:

- Is a table the best way to present the data? Could they be listed in the text, or would a figure be better?
- Do the data in the table complement—rather than duplicate— what is in the text? (Try to avoid repetition as far as possible.)
- Have you referred to the table in the text?
- Do you have a brief, informative title?
- Have you explained what the numbers in the table refer to?
- Are the headings clear and positioned appropriately in relation to the numbers?

Preparing figures

As noted earlier, a well-designed figure can provide a wealth of information very economically. Although you should always use a figure if
you want to demonstrate a relationship, this is not the only occasion
when you might choose a graphic presentation. The data presented
in Table 4.2, for instance, could also be shown in a bar graph (Figure
4.2). This kind of graph is especially useful when you want to compare
the effects of different experimental treatments on a variable.

Figure 4.2

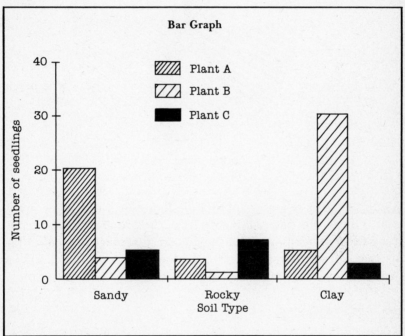

Or suppose that you have carried out a survey to determine how
students actually spent their time when they were "working" (you might
have asked a group of students to keep a diary of the amount of time
spent in various activities). You could present your data in a table,
simply listing the percentages of time spent doing different things,
but you would make the point of your findings much more emphati-
cally if you drew a pie chart (Figure 4.3). Here it is easy to see at a
glance that your sample group actually spent less than 50 per cent of
their "work time" doing things that might be construed as work.

Figure 4.3   **Pie Chart**

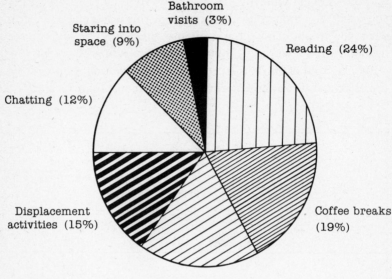

WORKTIME

Bathroom visits (3%)

Staring into space (9%)

Reading (24%)

Chatting (12%)

Displacement activities (15%)

Coffee breaks (19%)

Taking notes (18%)

In other cases the most appropriate figure might be a line graph such as the one on page 26 (Figure 4.1). There are many ways to present data graphically, and you should take advantage of them. A figure that is informative and well presented can make the difference between a mediocre grade and a good one.

Drawing graphs

You can make your graphs look very professional if you follow a few simple rules:

- Use a ruler and black ink. If you are not working in a lab book, consider drawing a rough version on graph paper and then tracing it onto plain paper.
- Place your independent variable (the one you have manipulated) on the horizontal axis (abscissa) and your dependent variable (the one you measure) on the vertical axis (ordinate).
- The ordinate should be about three-quarters of the length of the abscissa.

- Use large and distinctive symbols, with different symbols for each line on the graph.
- Label the axes clearly.
- Put in only essential detail. (A cluttered graph is difficult to read.)
- Include a legend to show what the different symbols represent.

There are many other refinements you could make, but even if you do no more than we have suggested here, your instructor will be favourably impressed. A well-organized and neatly presented Results section often reflects the quality of a student's work as a whole.

5
Documentation in the sciences

In psychology there is a uniform style for referring to the sources you have consulted. In the other sciences, however, the methods of documentation differ quite widely, even within a discipline. Always check with your instructor to make sure you are following the preferred practice for the course you are taking. Some instructors are very strict about citation practices; others will give you more freedom. The most important thing to remember is that your citations must be accurate.

A WARNING ABOUT PLAGIARISM

The main reason for citing other works in a paper is to tell readers about previous research on the topic and to let them know where you got your ideas from. If you put someone else's words or ideas down without acknowledging the source, that is a form of stealing.

Most universities have very severe penalties for plagiarism of any kind. The way to avoid even the suspicion of plagiarism is to give credit where it is due. If you are using someone else's ideas acknowledge them, even if you have changed the wording or just summarized the main points. The simplest way of giving credit is to cite your source in the text:

> The most likely explanation for this effect is . . . (Davis, 1979).

Don't be afraid that your paper will seem weaker if you acknowledge the ideas of others. On the contrary, it will be all the more convincing: virtually all scientific writing is based on previous work. Besides, citing the sources shows that you are aware of what has already been done.

Another and more serious form of plagiarism is to take not only another person's ideas, but his or her actual words, without acknowledgement. This is foolish as well as dishonest, because your instructor probably knows the literature much better than you do and may recognize the source. Even if the instructor does not recognize where the material came from, the style is often so different from the student's own that sections of plagiarized text are quite obvious.

If you do use someone else's words make it clear, either by enclosing them in quotation marks (if less than forty words), or by setting them off in a separate block of text with each line indented five spaces from the normal text margin. Give the source of the quotation, including the page number.

You don't need to acknowledge any idea or concept that has become common knowledge; for example, the helical structure of DNA or the Krebs cycle. But you should give credit for any idea that is neither well-known nor your own.

If you are writing a paper and encounter a single reference that presents a hypothesis consistent with your own thinking, acknowledge the work; don't try to pass the idea off as your own. And always document any fact or claim that is unfamiliar or open to question.

Styles of citation

Documentation in the sciences differs from that in the humanities in two important ways:

1. Instead of footnotes, there are brief references (citations) in the text itself.
2. Instead of a bibliography, there is a Reference section at the end of the paper, which lists only those works referred to directly in the text; other works are not listed.

There are two main styles of citation in scientific writing: alphabetical and consecutive. But within each style there are several different ways of citing the references in the text. The format of the work listed in the Reference section also varies enormously. This chapter will show you the most common citation formats and suggest journals that you may use as your models.

ALPHABETICAL LISTING

The most widely used alphabetical system is that suggested by the American Psychological Association in its manual (1983). Virtually all psychological publications, as well as a large number in the social sciences and other disciplines, use the APA format. This is our model (and the style used in this handbook).

Citation in the text

1. Author-date format. Here, the author's surname and the year of publication are inserted into the text at the appropriate point:

> Birchmore (1983) studied the children of alcoholics . . .
>
> Studies of children of alcoholics (Birchmore, 1983; Richards, 1978) have shown . . .
>
> In 1983, Birchmore reported . . .

2. Multiple authors. If there are two authors, always cite both names every time you cite the reference in the text. Use an ampersand (&) when the names are in parentheses, but use *and* in the running text:

> Newborn infants will orient better to high-frequency than low-frequency sounds (Morrongiello & Clifton, 1984), although Leventhal and Lipsitt (1964) found that neonates did not differentiate small frequency differences.

If there are more than two authors, cite all the names when the reference first occurs, and afterwards cite only the first author, followed by *et al.*:

> O'Day et al. (1981) investigated this autoinhibitor of zygote giant cell formation.

3. Organization of citations within parentheses. If you cite more than one item in a single set of parentheses, arrange them as follows:

1. Several papers by a single author ordered chronologically:

   (Smith, 1969, 1973, 1980, in press)

2. Several papers by the same author in the same year ordered with suffixes *a*, *b*, *c*, etc. after the year:

   (Smith, 1982a, 1982b)

3. Several papers by different authors in alphabetical order according to first author's surname:

(Aardvark, 1984; Smith, 1982a, 1982b; Zebra, 1932)

4. Referring to a specific part of a source. When referring to a particular item in a source, always give the specific location. When you quote a source, always give the page number:

(Smith, 1980, Fig. 2)

(Aslin, Alberts, & Petersen, 1982, p. 26)

5. Citing a reference you have not read. Although in general you should cite only works that you have read, occasionally you may want to cite something you haven't seen yourself, perhaps because it was not available. In that case refer to the work that cites it by adding a note (*as cited in* . . .) to the citation:

(Brown, 1979, as cited in Smith, 1981, p. 45)

6. Numerical citations. An alternative to the author-date citation is the numerical citation. A number of biological and medical journals use this style. Here the source is cited as a number that corresponds to the reference listed in the Reference section. Because the references are listed alphabetically in the Reference section, the citation numbers in the text cannot be assigned until all the references have been collated. If you take out or add any references, you will need to change the citation numbers. When this kind of numerical citation is used, the cited references are set either in parentheses or as superscripts in the appropriate places.

Several authors have described this phenomenon (18, 23, 31).

Several authors have described this phenomenon.[18, 23, 31]

Citation in the Reference section

Although sources are always cited alphabetically in the Reference section, the details vary across disciplines (see the sample entries below). Here are the general rules and exceptions:

1. The references are listed alphabetically. Begin with the first author's surname followed by his or her initials.

2. If there is more than one author, list all the names. (In some biological journals only the first three authors are listed.) Depending on the discipline, subsequent authors' initials either precede or follow their surnames.

3. When citing more than one work by a particular author, list the entries in chronological order. For works published in the same year, add the letter suffix (1982a, etc.) as you did in the text.

4. When the author is the publisher (as in the case of the manuals cited at the end of this chapter), the word *Author* takes the place of the publisher's name at the end of the citation.

5. The references are numbered only if you are using a numerical citation system.

6. Most often the full title of the publication is given, but in some cases it is omitted.

7. In some references to journals the name of the journal is abbreviated; in others it is not. But you must always give the volume and page numbers.

Sample entries

Psychology. Authors' initials always follow their surnames. The date of publication follows the author list. The titles of books and journals are underlined, as are the volume numbers of the journals. Journal titles are not abbreviated. Further details for citing different kinds of work are available in the *Publication Manual* of the American Psychological Association (1983).

Journal:

> King, F.L., & Kimura, D. (1972). Left-ear superiority in dichotic perception of vocal nonverbal sounds. Canadian Journal of Psychology, 26, 111–116.

Book:

> Lerner, R.M., & Hultsch, D.F. (1983). Human development: A life-span perspective. New York: McGraw-Hill.

Biology and the biomedical sciences. There is not a single standard format for the references in biological journals, although you can find some general rules in the *CBE Style Manual* (1983). Typically, journal names are abbreviated; for the accepted forms, see the 1976 *Biosis List of Serials*. Sometimes both the first and last pages of the reference are given and sometimes the last is not; placement of the year of publication, and details of punctuation, also vary across journals in different disciplines. The *Canadian Journal of Zoology* is used as a model here, but you should check with your instructor for the requirements in your course.

Journal:

> BURTON, M.P., and D.R. IDLER. 1984. The reproductive cycle of the winter flounder, Pseudopleuronectes americanus (Walbaum). Can. J. Zool. 62: 2563–2567.

Book:

> WHYTE, M.A. 1975. Time, tide and the cockle. In Growth rhythms and the history of the earth's rotation. Edited by G.D. Rosenberg and S.K. Runcorn. John Wiley and Sons, London. pp. 177–189.

CONSECUTIVE LISTING

Citation in the text

Another form of numerical citation found in biological and biomedical journals cites the sources consecutively in the text and in the Reference section. As before, the citations appear either in parentheses or as superscripts:

> Several authors have described this phenomenon.[1, 2, 3]

After the first citation use the same number whenever you refer to the same source.

Citation in the Reference section

The listing of the references in the Reference section is similar to that for the alphabetical system except that the references are placed in order of their first appearance in the text. Each reference is numbered. Although there is no standard form of reference, many biomedical journals have adopted what has come to be known as the Vancouver style (a format agreed upon by a number of editors of biomedical journals at a conference in Vancouver in 1978). Here are two sample entries:

Journal:

1. Moushegian G, Rupert AL, Langford TL. Stimulus coding by medial superior olivary neurons. J Neurophysiol 1967; 30:1239–1261.

Book:

2. Kuffler SW, Nicholls JG, Martin RA. From Neuron to Brain. 2nd edn. Sunderland, Mass. Sinauer Associates, 1984.

REFERENCES

American Psychological Association. (1983). *Publication manual of the American Psychological Association*. (3rd ed.). Washington, DC: Author.

Council of Biological Editors. (1983). *CBE style manual. A guide for authors, editors, and publishers in the biological sciences*. (5th ed.). Bethesda, MD.: Author.

6
Writing a research
paper

Students in the humanities get a lot of practice at writing essays of
one kind or another throughout their university careers, but those in
science may not. In psychology, instructors in upper-level courses will
often ask their classes to write research papers, only to hear several
students confess that they have never written an essay paper. If you
are one of the many students who dread writing an academic essay or
research paper, you will find that following a few simple steps in planning and organizing will make the task easier — and the result better.

Although there are many similarities between writing an essay in
English or history and one in psychology or biology, there are also
some differences. In particular, a scientific essay usually requires extensive citation of a body of literature, either to present what is known
about a particular topic or to support the thesis of the essay. The
trick to writing a good scientific essay is to organize your material
well and to provide a good story-line. Try to avoid the kind of paper
that is nothing more than an annotated bibliography of the papers
you have read: "Smith (1966) studied . . .; In 1973, Jones reported
. . .; An interesting result was obtained by Griffiths and Wilson (1981)";
and so on. Such a paper is tedious to read and often difficult to follow. Remember that a good style is just as important in scientific
writing as it is in English — take a look at the essays of Lewis Thomas
in *The Lives of a Cell* (1974) for an example of what scientific writing can be.

Before you worry about style, however, you need to think carefully
about what you are going to write.

THE PLANNING STAGE

Some students claim they can write essays without any planning at all. On the rare occasions when they succeed, their writing is usually not as spontaneous as it seems: almost certainly, they have thought or talked a good deal about the subject in advance and come to the task with some ready-made ideas. More often, trying to write a lengthy paper without planning just leads them to frustration. They get stuck in the middle and don't know how to finish, or suddenly realize that they are rambling off in all directions.

In contrast, most writers say that the planning, or pre-writing, stage is the most important part of the whole process. Certainly the evidence shows that poor planning usually leads to disorganized writing; in the majority of students' papers the single greatest improvement would not be better research or better grammar, but better organization.

This insistence on planning doesn't rule out exploratory writing (see p. 46). Many people find that the act of writing itself is the best way to generate ideas or overcome writer's block; the hard decisions about organization come after they've put something down on the page. Whether you organize before or after you begin to write, though, at some point you need to plan.

Reading primary material

In Chapter 2 we discussed how you might go about finding the relevant references in your field. Once you have done that you should begin reading through some of the original papers on your topic. Primary material is the direct evidence — usually journal articles and sometimes books — on which you will base your own paper. Surprising as it may seem, the best way to begin working with this material is to give it a fast initial skim. Don't just start reading every article from beginning to end. Read the Introduction sections of several papers to get a sense of the kinds of questions that the authors are asking. Getting an overview will allow you to focus your own questions for a more purposeful and analytic second reading. Make no mistake: a superficial reading is not all you need. You will have to work through the material carefully a second time. But an initial skim followed by a focused second reading will give you a much more thorough understanding than one slow plod ever will.

Some advice about secondary sources

In disciplines such as English, history, or philosophy, instructors may discourage secondary reading because they know the dangers of relying too heavily on it. If students turn to commentaries as a way around the difficulty of understanding primary material, they may be overwhelmed by the weight of authority, and their essays may be trite and second-hand. In the sciences, however, your first task is to find out what been written about your particular subject. Under these circumstances, judicious use of review articles or chapters can be a good way of getting a quick overview of your topic. Secondary sources can never substitute for your own active reading of the primary material, but they can serve a useful purpose.

Analyse your subject: ask questions

Some instructors ask students to choose their own paper topics, and others simply suggest subject areas. In either case, any subject area is bound to be too broad for a single paper. You will have to analyse it in order to ask questions that will lead to useful answers.

How do you form that kind of question? The most successful strategy here is to try to find a logically distinct sub-area of your major topic area that will be manageable in the length allowed for your paper and the time available. For example, if your general topic is "neural plasticity," you have an enormous number of possibilities for paper topics. You might begin by drawing a tree diagram of some of these possibilities, as shown in Figure 6.1.

Figure 6.1

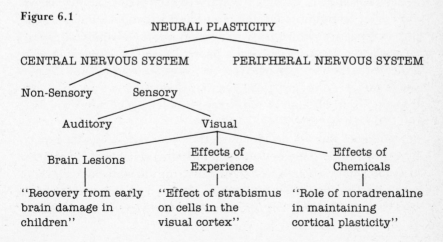

Obviously there are many more options than this, and some of the topic areas may overlap, but such a diagram can help you to decide what to include and what to leave out.

Analysing a prescribed topic

Even if the topic of your paper is supplied by your instructor, you still need to analyse it carefully. Try underlining key words to make sure that you don't neglect anything. Distinguish the main focus from subordinate concerns. A common error in dealing with prescribed topics is to emphasize one portion while giving short shrift to another. Give each part its proper due—and make sure you do what the instructions tell you to do. To *discuss* is not the same as to *evaluate* or to *trace*; to *compare* means to show differences as well as similarities. These verbs tell you how to approach the topic; don't confuse them. If the topic has been given in the form of a question, you may assume that the instructor wants you to answer that question, not one of your own devising.

Develop a theme

Not all scientific essays are arguments; often the purpose is simply to summarize the results of a number of research papers. Nevertheless, many students find it helpful to think of an academic essay as a way of demonstrating or proving a point, since the argumentative form is the easiest to organize and the most likely to produce forceful writing. It is not always necessary to develop a formal hypothesis, particularly if you are writing a review paper. Instead, you should develop a theme that will serve to hold together your information and ideas as you organize. As you progress, you may find that you want to change direction, but this kind of refinement is only possible after you have decided on a starting-point.

Sometimes you will decide to upgrade your theme into an explicit hypothesis to be presented in your introduction. Even if you never state it formally, though, you should take time to work out your thesis carefully. Use a complete sentence to express it and, above all, make sure that it is *limited, unified,* and *exact* (see McCrimmon, 1976).

Make it limited

A limited theme is one that is narrow enough to be workable. Suppose, for example, that your general subject is sexuality and adolescence. Such a subject is much too broad to be dealt with in an essay of one or two thousand words; you must limit it in some way and create a line of argument for which you can provide adequate supporting evidence. Using the analysis procedure described above, you might decide to limit your paper to attitudes about sex: "Over the past thirty years, adolescents' attitudes towards sex have changed from being very conservative to being very liberal and back again." Or you might prefer to limit it to a discussion of contraceptive use: "The availability of the birth-control pill and other contraceptives has led to an increased level of sexual activity among high-school students."

Make it unified

To be unified, your thesis must have one controlling idea. Beware of the double-headed thesis. For example, in a zoology essay on parasite-host interactions, your thesis might be something like this: "The decline of the seal hunt in Newfoundland has led to an increase in the number of parasitic worms found in codfish, but animal-rights groups are still receiving donations from people concerned about the death of baby seals." What is the controlling idea here? Is it the relations between the seals, the worms, and the codfish, or between the animal-rights groups and their benefactors? It is possible to have two or more related ideas in a thesis, but only if one of them is clearly in control, with all the other ideas subordinate to it: "Although it has been argued that studies of operant conditioning are not very useful, the principles developed from them are applied in many real-life situations."

Make it exact

It is important to avoid vague descriptive terms. Two of the worst are *interesting* and *significant*, as in "Banting and Best's early failures were significant steps towards their discovery of insulin." Were the failures significant because they provided an incentive for them to work harder, or because they provided insights that could be used later? Remember to be as specific as possible in creating your thesis, in order to focus your essay. Don't just make an assertion—give the main reasons for it. Instead of saying simply that "Intensive planting practices can increase crop yields substantially," and leaving it at that, add an explanation: ". . . because the plants are positioned strategically to allow maximum use of the space available, while the leaf cover provides a living mulch that discourages the growth of weeds."

Creating an outline

Individual writers differ in their need for a formal plan. Some say they never have an outline, and others maintain they can't write without one; most fall somewhere in between. Since organization is such a common problem, though, it's a good idea to know how to draw up an effective plan. Of course, the exact form it takes will depend on the pattern you use to develop your ideas—whether you are defining, classifying, or comparing.

If you have special problems with organizing material, your outline should be formal, in complete sentences. On the other hand, if your mind is naturally logical you may find it's enough just to jot down a few words on a scrap of paper. For most students, an informal but well-organized outline in point form is the most useful model:

Theme: "Because of their importance for survival, refined navigational skills are found throughout the animal kingdom. These skills are based on a wide variety of different cues."

   I. Orienting and navigating seen in many different kinds of animal.

   A. Birds
      1. Arctic tern
      2. Homing pigeon

   B. Insects
      1. Army ants
      2. Monarch butterfly

   C. Fish
      1. Salmon

   II. Navigating serves different purposes

   A. Migration
      1. Favourable climate
      2. Food availability
      3. Breeding grounds

      B. Locating local food sources
         1. Honeybee

III. Navigating animals use different cues.

      A. Celestial cues
         1. Sun-compass
         2. Star navigation

      B. Terrestrial cues
         1. Geomagnetism
         2. Barometric pressure
         3. Odour trails
         4. Landmarks

The guidelines for this kind of outline are simple:

Code your categories. Use different sets of markings to establish the relative importance of your entries. The example here moves from roman numerals, to letters, to arabic numbers, but you could use another system.

Categorize according to importance. Make sure that only items of equal value are put in equivalent categories. Give major points more weight than minor ones.

Check lines of connection. Make sure that each of the main categories is directly linked to the central thesis; then see that each subcategory is directly linked to the larger category that contains it. Checking these lines of connection is the best way of preventing essay muddle.

Be consistent. In arranging your points, be consistent. You may choose to move from the most important point to the least important, or vice versa, as long as you follow the same order every time.

Use parallel wording. Phrasing each entry in a similar way will make it easier to be consistent in your presentation.

One final word: be prepared to change your outline at any time in the writing process. An outline is not meant to put an iron clamp on your thinking, but to relieve anxiety about where you're heading. A careful outline prevents frustration and dead ends—that "I'm stuck, where can I go from here?" feeling. But since the very act of writing will usually generate new ideas, you should be ready to modify your original plan. Just remember that any new outline must have the consistency and clear connections required for a unified essay.

THE WRITING STAGE

Writing the first draft

Few writers labour for excellence from scratch; most find it easier to write the first draft as quickly as possible and do extensive revisions later. However you begin, you can't expect the first draft to be the final copy. Skilled writers know that revising is a necessary part of the writing process, and that the care taken with revisions makes the difference between a mediocre essay and a good one.

You don't need to write all parts of the essay in the same order in which they are to appear in the final copy. In fact, many students find the introduction the hardest part to write. If you face the first blank page with a growing sense of paralysis, try leaving the introduction until later, and start with the first idea in your outline. If you feel so intimidated that you haven't even been able to draw up an outline, you might try John Trimble's approach and charge right ahead with any kind of beginning—even a simple "My first thoughts on this subject are . . ." (Trimble, 1975, p. 11). Instead of sharpening pencils or running out for a snack, try to get going. Don't worry about grammar or wording; scratch out pages or throw them away if you must. Remember, the object is to get your writing juices flowing.

Of course, you can't expect this kind of exploratory writing to resemble the first draft that follows an outline. You will probably need to do a great deal more changing and reorganizing, but at least you will have the relief of seeing words on a page to work with. Many experienced writers—and not only those with writer's block—find this the most productive way to proceed.

Developing your ideas: some common patterns

The way you develop your ideas will depend on your topic, and topics can vary enormously. Even so, most research papers follow one of a few basic organizational patterns. Here's how to use each pattern effectively.

1. Defining

Sometimes a whole paper is an extended definition, explaining the meaning of a concept that is complicated, controversial, or simply important to your field of study: for example, the *superego* in psychoanalytic writings, *prions* in microbiology, or *evolution* in biology. More often you may want to begin a detailed discussion of a topic by defining a key term, and then shift to a different organizational pattern. In either case, make your definition exact. It should be broad enough to include all the things that belong in the category and at the same time narrow enough to exclude things that don't belong. A good definition builds a kind of verbal fence around a concept, herding together all the members of the class and cutting off all outsiders.

For any discussion of a term that goes beyond a bare definition, of course, you should give concrete illustrations or examples; depending on the nature of your paper, these could vary in length from one or two sentences to several paragraphs or even pages. If you are defining the superego, for instance, you will probably want to discuss at some length the theories of leading psychoanalysts.

In an extended definition, it's also useful to point out the differences between the term and any other that is connected with it or often confused with it. For instance, if you are defining prions you might want to distinguish them from viruses; if you are defining a modern version of evolutionary theory, you should contrast it with classical Darwinian theory.

2. Classifying

Classifying means dividing something into its separate parts according to a given principle of selection. The principle or criterion may vary. You could classify crops, for example, according to how they grow (above the ground or below the ground), how long they take to mature, or what climatic conditions they require; the population of an ecological niche might be classified according to species present, distribution within the niche, degree of interdependence, and so on. If you are organizing your essay by a system of classification, remember the following:

- All members of a class must be accounted for. If any are left over, you need to alter some categories or add more.
- Categories can be divided into subcateogries. You should consider using subcategories if there are significant differences within a category. For instance, if you are classifying the effects of brain damage according to the site of the lesion, you might want to

create subcategories according to effects: memory deficits, language problems, perceptual difficulties, and so on.
- Any subcategory should contain at least two items.

3. Explaining a process

This kind of organization shows how something works or has worked, whether it be the weather cycle, the photochemical reactions of the eye, or the mechanisms of hibernation. The important point to remember is to be systematic, to break down the process into a series of steps or stages. Although the order will vary depending upon the circumstances, most often it will be chronological, in which case you should see that the sequence is accurate and easy to follow. Whatever the arrangement, you can generally make the process easier to follow if you start a new paragraph for each new stage.

4. Tracing causes or effects

A cause-or-effect analysis is really a particular kind of process discussion, in which certain events are shown to have led to or resulted from other events. Usually you are explaining why something happened. The main warning here is to avoid over-simplifying. If you are tracing causes, distinguish between a direct cause and a contributing cause, between what is a condition of something happening and what is merely a correlation or coincidence. For example, if you discover that there is a high correlation between the number of garbage dumps and the number of polar bears sighted around Churchill, Manitoba, you should not conclude that the bears breed in the garbage dumps. You must be sure that the result you mention is a genuine product of the event or action in question.

5. Comparing

One point sometimes forgotten is that comparing things means showing differences as well as similarities — even if the topic does not say *compare and contrast*. The easiest method for comparison — though not always the best — is to discuss the first subject in the comparison thoroughly and then move on to the second:

        Subject X: Point 1
                    Point 2
                    Point 3

```
Subject Y:  Point 1
            Point 2
            Point 3
```

The problem with this kind of comparison is that it often sounds like two separate essays slapped together. To be successful you must integrate the two subjects, first in your introduction, by putting them both in a single context, and again in your conclusion, where you should bring together the important points you have made about each. When discussing the second subject, try to refer repeatedly to your findings about the first subject ("unlike x, y does such and such"). This method may be the wisest choice if the subjects for comparison seem so unlike that it is hard to create similar categories in which to place them for discussion—if the points you are making about x are of a different type from the points you are making about y.

If it is possible to find similar criteria or categories for discussing both subjects, however, the comparison will be more effective if you organize it like this:

```
Category 1:  Subject x
             Subject y
Category 2:  Subject x
             Subject y
Category 3:  Subject x
             Subject y
```

Because this kind of comparison is more tightly integrated, the reader can more readily see the similarities and differences between the subjects. As a result, the essay is likely to be more forceful.

Introductions

The beginning of a research paper has a dual purpose: to indicate both the topic and your approach to it, and to whet your reader's appetite for what you have to say. One effective way of introducing a topic is to place it in a context—to supply a kind of backdrop that will put it in perspective. You step back a pace and discuss the area into which your topic fits, and then gradually lead into your specific field of discussion. Baker (1981, pp. 24-5) calls this the "funnel approach." For example, suppose that your topic is the specific action of certain neurotoxins on the nervous system. You might begin with a more general discussion of the effects of some of the naturally occurring neurotoxins, such as that produced by the pufferfish. The funnel opening is applicable to almost any kind of paper.

It's a good idea to try to catch your reader's interest right from the start—you know from your own reading how a dull beginning can put you off. The fact that your instructor must read on anyway makes no difference. If a reader has to get through thirty or forty similar essays, it's all the more important for yours to stand out. A funnel opening isn't the only way to catch the reader's attention. Here are three of the most common leads:

The quotation. This approach works especially well when the quotation is taken from the person or work that you will be discussing.

The question. A rhetorical question will only annoy the reader if it's commonplace or the answer is obvious, but a thought-provoking question can make a strong opening. Just be sure that you answer the question in your essay.

The anecdote or telling fact. This is the kind of concrete lead that journalists often use to grab their readers' attention. Because it can convey an unwanted sense of flippancy, it is rarely used in scientific writing. Save it for your least formal essays—and remember that the incident must really highlight the ideas you are going to discuss.

Whatever your lead, it must relate to your topic: never sacrifice relevance for originality. Finally, whether your introduction is one paragraph or several, make sure that by the end of it your reader clearly knows the direction you are taking.

Conclusions

Endings can be painful—sometimes for the reader as much as for the writer. Too often, the feeling that one ought to say something profound and memorable produces an ending that is either pompous or meaningless. You know the sort of thing:

> This is not to say that the research of the last decade has been in vain, to the contrary, we have learned a tremendous amount. Critical and conflicting evidence does tell us however, that we still have a long way to go before we can deal in absolutes. (Student essay, 1985)

Even if you ignore the grammatical difficulties, you can see that these last two sentences might better have been left unwritten.

Experienced editors often say that many articles and essays would be better without their final paragraphs: in other words, when you have finished what you want to say, the only thing to do is stop. This advice works best for short papers where you need to keep the central point firmly in the foreground and don't need to remind the reader of it. For longer pieces, where you have developed a number of ideas or a complex line of argument, you should provide a sense of closure. Readers welcome an ending that helps to tie the ideas together; they don't like to feel they've been left dangling. And since the final impression is often the most lasting, it's in your interest to finish strongly. Simply restating your thesis or summarizing what you have already said isn't forceful enough. What are the other options?

The inverse funnel. The simplest and most basic conclusion is one that restates the thesis in different words and then discusses its implications. Baker (1981, pp. 24-5) calls this the "inverse funnel approach," as opposed to the funnel approach of the opening paragraph. One danger in moving to a wider perspective is that you may try to embrace too much. When a conclusion expands too far it tends to lose focus and turn into an empty cliché, like the conclusion in the preceding example. It's always better to discuss specific implications than to leap into the thin air of vague generalities.

The new angle. A variation of the basic inverse funnel approach is to reintroduce your argument with a new twist. Suggesting some fresh angle can add excitement to your ending. Beware of injecting an entirely new idea, though, or one that's only loosely connected to your original argument: the result could be jarring or even off-topic.

The full circle. If your introduction is based on an anecdote, a question, or a startling fact, you can complete the circle by referring to it again in relation to some of the insights revealed in the main body of your essay.

The stylistic flourish. Some of the most successful conclusions end on a strong stylistic note. Try varying the sentence structure: if most of your sentences are long and complex, make the last one short and punchy, or vice versa. Sometimes you can dramatize your idea with a striking phrase or colourful image. When you are writing your essay, keep your eyes open and your ears tuned for fresh ways of putting things, and save the best for the end.

None of these approaches to endings is exclusive, of course. You may even find that several of them can be combined in a single essay.

THE EDITING STAGE

Often the best writer in a class is not the one who can dash off a fluent first draft, but the one who is the best editor. To edit your work well you need to see it as the reader will; you have to distinguish between what you meant to say and what is actually on the page. For this reason it's a good idea to leave some time between drafts, so that when you begin to edit you will be looking at the writing afresh rather than reviewing it from memory. Now is the time to go to a movie or play some squash—do anything that will take your mind off your work. Without this distancing period you can become so involved that it's hard to see your paper objectively.

Editing doesn't mean simply checking your work for errors in grammar or spelling. It means looking at the piece as a whole to see if ideas are (1) well-organized, (2) well-documented, and (3) well-expressed. It may mean adding some paragraphs, deleting others, and shifting still others around. It very likely means adding, deleting, and shifting sentences and phrases. Experienced writers may be able to check several aspects of their work at the same time, but if you are inexperienced or in doubt about your writing, it's best to look at the organization of the ideas before you tackle sentence structure, diction, style, and documentation. As you read through your paper, ask yourself whether it flows properly: is the rhythm comfortable, or do you find yourself slowed down by passages that are awkwardly constructed? Often such problems can be corrected simply by shifting the word order.

What follows is a check-list of questions to ask yourself as you begin editing. Far from being all-inclusive, it focuses on the first step: examining the organization. You probably won't want to check through your work separately for each question: you can group some together and overlook others, depending on your own strengths and weaknesses as a writer.

Preliminary editing check-list

1. Are the purpose and approach of this essay evident from the beginning?

2. Are all sections of the paper relevant to the topic?
3. Is the organization logical?
4. Are the ideas sufficiently developed? Is there enough evidence, explanation, and illustration?
5. Would an educated person who hasn't read the primary material understand everything I'm saying? Should I clarify some parts or add any explanatory material?
6. In presenting my argument, do I take into account opposing arguments or evidence?
7. Do my paragraph divisions give coherence to my ideas? Do I use them to cluster similar ideas and signal changes of ideas?
8. Do any parts of the paper seem disjointed? Should I add more transitional words or logical indicators to make the sequence of ideas easier to follow?

Another approach would be to devise your own check-list based on the faults of previous assignments. This is particularly useful when you move from the overview to the close focus on sentence structure, diction, punctuation, spelling, and style. If you have a particular weak area—for example, irrelevant evidence, faulty logic, or run-on sentences—you should give it special attention. Keeping a personal check-list will save you from repeating the same old mistakes.

A few words about appearance

We've all been told not to judge a book by its cover, but the very warning suggests that we have a natural tendency to do so. Readers of student papers find the same thing. A well-typed, visually appealing essay creates a receptive reader and, fairly or unfairly, often gets a higher mark than a handwritten one—especially if the handwriting is messy or hard to read. Whenever possible, therefore, type your essay. If you can't type or afford to hire a typist, take special care that your script is neat and easy to read. If your handwriting is poor, print. In any case, double-space your lines and leave wide margins on the sides, top, and bottom, framing the script in white. Leave three centimetres at least at the sides and top and four centimetres at the bottom, so that the reader has ample space to write comments. Number each page at the top right-hand corner, and provide a neat, well-spaced cover page that includes the title, your name, your instructor's name, and the number of your course. Good looks won't substitute for good thinking, but they will certainly enhance it.

USING A WORD-PROCESSOR

These days it is becoming more common to see student papers with the characteristic typeface of the dot matrix or—in rare cases—laser printer. The advent of the computer and relatively inexpensive, easy-to-use word-processing packages has made a tremendous difference to the way people write. The word-processor can be a wonderful tool to assist you in your writing—if you use it judiciously.

Using a word-processor does not mean "getting into computers"; most word-processing systems simply make your computer keyboard into a fancy typewriter that allows you to correct mistakes before they arrive on paper, rearrange your material for ease of reading, and print out a neat and tidy final copy. Most systems are easy to learn and they can speed up your writing considerably. To some extent they can also help you to improve your writing skills, because they make it easier for you to revise—to add, delete, or correct, change passages, or move paragraphs around. Here are a few simple suggestions that might be useful if you have, or are thinking of getting, a computer to do word-processing.

1. Type your material directly into the computer

The traditional way of writing a paper that eventually will be typed is to write it out in longhand, and then type it or have someone else type it for you. You can speed up the physical writing process enormously by typing your paper directly into the computer. Even if you can't type very well, it doesn't really matter; when you are writing a paper, the time spent thinking will far outweigh the time it takes to enter the words into the computer. A common argument against writing in this fashion is "I can't think at the typewriter." But once you try, you may find it's rewarding. Seeing your thoughts appearing in a legible form in front of you will help keep you going.

2. Try different ways of organizing your paper

Perhaps the most useful aspect of a word-processing system is that it allows you to move blocks of text around so that you can try out different ways of organizing your paper. If you have ever reached the point where your handwritten version has become so complicated that you have to rewrite the whole thing out in order to make any sense of it, you will appreciate being able to make on-screen corrections and rearrangements. You can set up a new organizational structure for your paper and if, after reading it through, you don't like it, you can always go back to your original version.

3. Don't let the system rule your thinking

Seeing something typed out neatly on a screen or on paper makes it seem more acceptable than messy handwriting, even though the quality of the work may be no different. Don't be fooled into thinking that quality typing replaces quality thinking. Read over your work with a critical eye, in the knowledge that you can easily change something that is unsatisfactory. Remember that the word-processor is a tool for you to use — no more than that.

4. Save regularly and back up your files

If you are used to working with a computer, you know the importance of this advice; if not, take it to heart. There is nothing more agonizing than to discover that something has gone wrong and caused you to lose everything you have been working on. It doesn't happen very often, but everyone experiences it at least once, and always unexpectedly. There is one easy way around the problem: when you are writing, save your work file every fifteen minutes or so. Then when your room-mate pulls the plug on the computer to turn on the TV, the most you will lose is the typing you have done since you last saved your file. A potentially more serious problem may arise if your cat decides to find out what computer disks taste like, or if you are careless with a cup of coffee. Again, a little foresight will save you from losing everything. As soon as you have completed a section of work, make a copy of it on another disk and keep it well away from the computer. An up-to-date back-up system like this will spare you a lot of frustration.

Word-processors are not the answer to all your writing needs, but if you are thinking about getting an electric typewriter, you might consider buying an inexpensive computer instead. It will do a lot more for you — and besides, you can always play video games when the strain of writing becomes too much.

REFERENCES

Baker, S. (1981). *The practical stylist* (5th ed., pp. 24–5). New York: Harper & Row.

McCrimmon, J. (1976). *Writing with a purpose* (6th ed., p. 18). Boston: Houghton Mifflin.

Thomas, L. (1974). *Lives of a cell: Notes of a biology watcher.* New York: Viking Press.

Trimble, J.R. (1975). *Writing with style: Conversations on the art of writing* (p. 11). Englewood Cliffs, NJ: Prentice-Hall.

7
Writing with style

As we mentioned in the previous chapter, style is just as important in scientific writing as it is in any other kind, especially when you realize that writing with style does not mean stuffing your prose with fancy words and extravagant images. Any style, from the simplest to the most elaborate, can be effective, depending on the occasion and intent. Writers known for their style are those who have projected something of their own personality into their writing; we can hear a distinctive voice in what they say. It will take time to develop your own style, but in the meantime just remember that the most effective style for scientific writing is one that is clear, concise, and forceful.

BE CLEAR

Since sentence structure is dealt with in Chapter 9, this section will focus on clear wording and paragraphing.

Choosing clear words

A good dictionary is a wise investment; get into the habit of using one. It will give you not only common meanings, but less familiar applications and derivations, as well as proper spelling. Canadian usage and spelling may follow either British or American practices, but usually combine aspects of both; you should check before you buy a dictionary to be sure that it gives these variants.

A thesaurus lists words that are closely related in meaning. It can help when you want to avoid repeating yourself, or when you're fumbling for a word that's on the tip of your tongue. But be careful: make sure you remember the difference between denotative and connotative meanings. A word's denotation is its primary or "dictionary" meaning. Its connotations are any associations that it may suggest;

they may not be as exact as the denotations, but they are part of the impression the word conveys. If you examine a list of "synonyms" in a thesaurus, you will see that even words with similar meanings can have dramatically different connotations. For example, alongside the word *indifferent* your thesaurus may give the following: *neutral, unconcerned, careless, easy-going, unambitious*, and *half-hearted*. Imagine the different impressions you would create if you chose one or the other of those words to complete this sentence: "Questioned about the experiment's chance of success, he was _____ in his response." In order to write clearly, you must remember that a reader may react to the suggestive meaning of a word as much as to its "dictionary" meaning.

1. Use plain English

Plain words are almost always more forceful than fancy ones. If you aren't sure what plain English is, think of everyday speech: how do you talk to your friends? Many of our most common words—the ones that sound most natural and direct—are short. A good number of them are also among the oldest words in the English language. By contrast, most of the words that English has derived from other languages are longer and more complicated; even after they've been used for centuries, they can still sound artificial. For this reason you should beware of words loaded with prefixes (*pre-, post-, anti-, pro-, sub-, maxi-,* etc.) and suffixes (*-ate, -ize, -tion,* etc.). These Latinate attachments can make individual words more precise and efficient, and are particularly useful for describing specific technical processes. Putting a lot of them together, however, will make your writing seem dense and hard to understand. In many cases you can substitute a plain word for a fancy one:

Fancy	*Plain*
determinant	cause
utilization	use
cognizant	aware
obviate	prevent
terminate	end
infuriate	anger
oration	speech
conclusion	end
requisite	needed

numerous	many
finalize	finish, complete
systematize	order
sanitize	clean
remuneration	pay
maximization	increase

Suggesting that you write in plain English does not mean that you should never pick an unfamiliar, long, or foreign word: sometimes those words are the only ones that will convey precisely what you mean, especially in a scientific paper. Inserting an unusual expression into a passage of plain writing can also be an effective means of catching the reader's attention—as long as you don't do it too often.

2. Be precise

Always be as precise or exact as you can. Avoid all-purpose adjectives like *major*, *significant*, and *important*, and vague verbs such as *involved*, *entail*, and *exist*, when you can be more specific:

orig. Catalysts are involved in many biochemical reactions.

rev. Catalysts speed up many biochemical reactions.

Here's another example:

orig. The discovery of genetic engineering techniques was a significant contribution to biological science.

rev. The discovery of genetic engineering techniques was a dangerous contribution to biological science.

(or)

rev. The discovery of genetic engineering techniques was a beneficial contribution to biological science.

3. Avoid unnecessary qualifiers

Qualifiers such as *very*, *rather*, and *extremely* are over-used. Saying that something is *very elegant* may have less impact than saying simply that it is *elegant*. For example, compare these sentences:

They devised an elegant hypothesis to explain their data.

They devised a very elegant hypothesis to explain their data.

Which has more punch?

When you think that an adjective needs qualifying—and sometimes it will—first see if it's possible to change either the adjective or the phrasing. Instead of writing:

orig. Multinational Drugs made a very big profit last year.

Write

rev. Multinational Drugs made an unprecedented profit last year.

or (if you aren't sure whether or not the profit actually set a record):

rev. Multinational Drugs' profit rose forty per cent last year.

In some cases qualifiers not only weaken your writing but are redundant, since the adjectives themselves are absolutes. To say that something is *very unique* makes as much—or as little—sense as to say that someone is *slightly pregnant* or *very dead*.

4. Avoid fancy jargon

One of the worst sins you can commit in scientific writing—and it is by no means confined to fledgling scientists—is the use of jargon that is unintelligible to the unitiated. "Never use a short word if a longer, more esoteric one will do" seems to be the unfortunate motto of many scientific writers. Although sometimes you must use special terms to avoid long and complex explanations, you should keep the rest of your paper in simple English. At first glance it may not appear so impressive, but it will certainly be a lot easier to read.

Creating clear paragraphs

Paragraphs come in so many sizes and patterns that no single formula could possibly cover them all. The two basic principles to remember are these: (1) a paragraph is a means of developing and framing an idea or impression, and (2) the divisions between paragraphs aren't random, but indicate a shift in focus.

1. Develop your ideas

You are not likely to sit down and consciously ask yourself, "What pattern shall I use to develop this paragraph?" What comes first is the idea you intend to develop: the pattern the paragraph takes should flow from the idea itself and the way you want to discuss or expand it.

(The most common ways of developing an idea are outlined on pp. 46–9.)

You may take one or several paragraphs to develop an idea fully. For a definition alone you could write one paragraph or ten, depending on the complexity of the subject and the nature of the assignment. Just remember that ideas need development, and that each new paragraph signals a change in idea.

2. Consider the topic sentence

Skilled skim-readers know that they can get the general drift of a book simply by reading the first sentence of each paragraph. The reason is that most paragraphs begin by stating the central idea to be developed. If you are writing your essay from a formal plan, you will probably find that each section and subsection will generate the topic sentence for a new paragraph.

Like the thesis statement for the paper as a whole, the topic sentence is not obligatory: in some paragraphs the controlling idea is not stated until the middle or even the end, and in others it is not stated at all but merely implied. Nevertheless, it's a good idea to think out a topic sentence for every paragraph. That way you'll be sure that each one has a readily graspable point and is clearly connected to what comes before and after. When revising your initial draft, check to see that each paragraph is held together by a topic sentence, either stated or implied. If you find that you can't formulate one, you should probably rework the whole paragraph.

3. Maintain focus

To be clear, a paragraph should contain only those details that are in some way related to the central idea. It must also be structured so that the details are easily seen to be related. One way of showing these relations is to keep the same grammatical subject in most of the sentences that make up the paragraph. When the grammatical subject is shifting all the time, a paragraph loses focus, as in the following example (based on Cluett & Ahlborn, 1965, p. 51):

> Boys in school play a variety of sports these days. In the fall, football still attracts the most, although an increasing number now play soccer. For some basketball is the favourite when the ball season is over, but you will find that swimming or gymnastics are also popular. Cold winter temperatures may allow the school to have an outdoor rink, and

> then <u>hockey</u> becomes a source of enjoyment for many. In
> spring, though, the <u>rinks</u> begin melting, and so <u>there</u> is less
> opportunity to play. Then some <u>boys</u> take up soccer again,
> while <u>track and field</u> also attracts many participants.

Here the grammatical subject (underlined) is constantly jumping from
one thing to another. Notice how much stronger the focus becomes
when all the sentences have the same grammatical subject — either
the same noun, a synonym, or a related pronoun:

> <u>Boys</u> in school play a variety of sports these days. In the
> fall, <u>most</u> still choose football, although an increasing <u>num-</u>
> <u>ber</u> now play soccer. When the ball season is over, <u>some</u> turn
> to basketball; <u>others</u> prefer swimming or gymnastics. If cold
> winter temperatures permit an outdoor rink, many <u>boys</u>
> enjoy hockey. Once the ice begins to melt in spring, though,
> <u>they</u> can play less often. Then <u>some</u> take up soccer again,
> while <u>others</u> choose track and field.

Naturally it's not always possible to retain the same grammatical
subject throughout a paragraph. If you were comparing the athletic
pursuits of boys and girls, for example, you would have to switch back
and forth between boys and girls as your grammatical subject. In the
same way, you will have to shift when you are discussing examples of
an idea or exceptions to it.

4. Avoid monotony

If most or all of the sentences in your paragraph have the same grammatical subject, how do you avoid boring your reader? There are two
easy ways:

Use stand-in words. Pronouns, either personal (*I, we, you, he, she,
it, they*) or demonstrative (*this, that, those*) can stand in for the subject, as can synonyms (words or phrases that mean the same thing).
The revised paragraph on boys' sports, for example, uses the pronouns *some, most,* and *they* as substitutes for boys. Most well-written
paragraphs have a liberal sprinkling of these stand-in words.

"Bury" the subject by putting something in front of it. When the
subject is placed in the middle of the sentence rather than at the beginning, it's less obvious to the reader. If you take another look at the
revised paragraph, you'll see that in several sentences there is a word

or phrase in front of the subject, such as *first*, *then*, *lately*, or *moreover*. (Incidentally, this is a useful technique to remember when you are writing a letter of application and want to avoid starting every sentence with *I*.)

5. Link your ideas

To create coherent paragraphs, you need to link your ideas clearly. Linking words are those connectors—conjunctions and conjunctive adverbs—that show the relations between one sentence, or part of a sentence, and another; they're also known as transition words, because they bridge the transition from one thought to another. Make a habit of using linking words when you shift from one grammatical subject or idea to another, whether the shift occurs within a single paragraph or as you move from one paragraph to the next. Here are some of the most common connectors and the logical relations they indicate:

Linking Word	*Logical Relation*
and also again further in addition similarly likewise more moreover	addition to previous idea
but although despite however in spite of nevertheless rather yet by contrast on the other hand even so	change from previous idea

accordingly
consequently
hence
so   } summary or conclusion
therefore
thus
for this reason

Numerical terms such as *first*, *second*, and *third* also work well as links.

6. Vary the length, but avoid extremes

Ideally, academic writing will have a comfortable balance of long and short paragraphs. Avoid the extremes, especially the one-sentence paragraph that can only state an idea, without explaining or developing it. A series of very short paragraphs is usually a sign that you have not developed your ideas in enough detail, or that you have started new paragraphs unnecessarily. On the other hand, a succession of long paragraphs can be tiring and difficult to read. In deciding when to start a new paragraph, remember always to consider what is clearest and most helpful for the reader.

BE CONCISE

At one time or another, you will probably be tempted to pad your writing. Whatever the reason—because you need to write two or three thousand words and have only enough to say for one thousand, or just because you think length is strength and hope to get a better mark for the extra—padding is a mistake. You may fool some of the people some of the time, but not often.

Strong writing is always concise. It leaves out anything that does not serve some communicative or stylistic purpose, in order to say as much as possible in as few words as possible. Concise writing will help you do better on both your essays and your exams.

Guidelines for concise writing

1. Use adverbs and adjectives sparingly

Avoid the shotgun approach to adverbs and adjectives; don't just spray your work with modifiers in the hope that one will hit. One well-chosen word is always better than a series of synonyms:

orig. As well as being <u>costly</u> and <u>financially extravagant</u>, the project is <u>reckless</u> and <u>foolhardy</u>.

rev. The venture is <u>foolhardy</u> as well as <u>costly</u>.

2. Avoid noun clusters

A recent trend in some writing is to use nouns as adjectives, as in the phrase *noun cluster*. This device can be effective occasionally, but frequent use can produce a monstrous pile-up of words. Breaking up noun clusters may not always produce fewer words, but it will make your writing easier to read:

orig. word-processor utilization manual

rev. manual for using word-processors

orig. pollution investigation committee

rev. committee to investigate pollution

3. Avoid chains of relative clauses

Sentences full of clauses beginning with *which, that,* or *who* are usually more wordy than necessary. Try reducing some of those clauses to phrases or single words:

orig. The solutions <u>that</u> were discussed last night have a practical benefit, <u>which</u> is easily grasped by people <u>who</u> have no technical training.

rev. The solutions discussed last night have a practical benefit, easily grasped by non-technical people.

4. Try reducing clauses to phrases or words

Independent clauses can often be reduced by subordination. Here are a few examples:

orig. The report was written in a clear and concise manner and it was widely read.

rev. Written in a clear and concise manner, the report was widely read.

rev. Clear and concise, the report was widely read.

orig. His plan was of a radical nature and was a source of embarrassment to his employer.

rev. His radical plan embarrassed his employer.

For more detail on subordination and reduction, see pp. 68-9.

5. Strike out hackneyed expressions and circumlocutions

Trite or roundabout phrases may flow from your pen without a thought, but they make for stale prose. Unnecessary words are deadwood; be prepared to hunt and chop ruthlessly to keep your writing vital:

Wordy	Revised
due to the fact that	because
at this point in time	now
consensus of opinion	consensus
in the near future	soon
when all is said and done	(omit)
in the eventuality that	if
in all likelihood	likely

6. Avoid "it is" and "there is" beginnings

Although it may not always be possible, try to avoid *it is* or *there is (are)* beginnings. Your sentences will be crisper and more concise:

orig There are only a few days in the year when the phenomenon occurs.

rev. The phenomenon occurs on only a few days of the year.

orig. It is certain that pollution will increase.

rev. Pollution will certainly increase.

BE FORCEFUL

Developing a forceful, vigorous style simply means learning some common tricks of the trade and practising them until they become habit.

1. Choose active over passive verbs

An active verb creates more energy than a passive one does:

>   Active: She wiped up the spill.

Passive: The spill was wiped up by her.

Moreover, passive constructions tend to produce awkward, convoluted phrasing. Writers of bureaucratic documents are among the worst offenders:

> It has been decided that the utilization of small rivers in the province for purposes of generating hydro-electric power should be studied by our department and that a report to the Deputy should be made by our Director as soon as possible.

The passive verbs in this mouthful make it hard to tell who is doing what.

Passive verbs are appropriate in two specific cases:

1. When the situation described is in fact passive — that is, when the subject of the sentence is the passive recipient of some action.
2. When using a passive verb will help to maintain focus by eliminating the need to shift to a different subject. The following example has both reasons for using the passive verb *were eaten*:

> The guppies had adjusted to their new tank but they were eaten by the larger fish a short time later.

2. Use personal subjects

Most of us find it more interesting to learn about people than about things — hence the enduring appeal of the gossip columns. Wherever possible, therefore, make the subjects of your sentences personal. This trick goes hand-in-hand with use of active verbs. Almost any sentence becomes more lively with active verbs and a personal subject:

orig. The materialistic implications of Darwin's theory led to a long delay before it was published.

rev. Darwin delayed publication of his theory for a long time because of its materialistic implications.

Here's another example:

orig. It may be concluded that the reaction had been permitted to continue until it was completed because there was no sign of any precipitate when the flask was examined.

rev. We may conclude that the reaction had finished because we could not see any precipitate when we examined the flask.

3. Use concrete details

Concrete details are easier to understand—and to remember—than abstract theories. Whenever you are discussing abstract concepts, therefore, always provide specific examples and illustrations; if you have a choice between a concrete word and an abstract one, choose the concrete. Consider this sentence:

> Watson and Crick were the first to demonstrate the helical structure of DNA.

Now see how a few specific details can bring the facts to life:

> Watson and Crick showed that the DNA molecule was arranged as a double helix and that this organization helped to explain how genes could be replicated.

Suggesting that you add concrete details doesn't mean getting rid of all abstractions. It's simply a plea to balance them with accurate details. This is one occasion when added wording, if it is concrete and correct, can improve your writing.

4. Make important ideas stand out

Experienced writers know how to manipulate sentences in order to emphasize certain points. Here are some of their techniques:

Place key words in strategic positions. The positions of emphasis in a sentence are the beginning and, above all, the end. If you want to bring your point home with force, don't put the key words in the middle of the sentence. Save them for the last:

orig. People are less afraid of losing wealth than of losing face in this image-conscious society.

rev. In this image-conscious society people are less afraid of losing wealth than of losing face.

Subordinate minor ideas. Small children connect incidents with a string of *and*s, as if everything were of equal importance:

> We went to the zoo and we saw a lion and John spilled his drink.

As they grow up, however, they learn to subordinate: that is, to make one part of a sentence less important in order to emphasize another point:

> Because there was little demand for his course, in the
> following year it was cancelled.
>   s   v

Major ideas stand out more and connections become clearer when
minor ideas are subordinated:

orig. Spring arrived and we had nothing to do.

rev. When spring arrived, we had nothing to do.

Make your most important idea the subject of the main clause, and
try to put it at the end, where it will be most emphatic:

orig. I was relieved when I saw my marks.

rev. When I saw my marks I was relieved.

Vary sentence structure. As with anything else, variety adds spice to
writing. One way of adding variety, which will also make an important idea stand out, is to use a periodic rather than a simple sentence
structure.

  Most sentences follow the simple pattern of subject — verb — object
(plus modifiers):

> The dog bit the man on the ankle.
>   s   v   o

A *simple sentence* such as this gives the main idea at the beginning
and therefore creates little tension. A *periodic sentence*, on the other
hand, does not give the main clause until the end, following one or
more subordinate clauses:

> Since there was little demand for his course, in the follow-
> ing year it was cancelled.
>   s   v

The longer the periodic sentence is, the greater the suspense and the
more emphatic the final part. Since this high-tension structure is more
difficult to read than the simple sentence, your readers would be
exhausted if you used it too often. Save it for those times when you
want to make a very strong point.

Vary sentence length. A short sentence can add punch to an important point, especially when it comes as a surprise. This technique
can be particularly useful for conclusions. Don't overdo it, though. A
string of long sentences may be monotonous, but a string of short
ones has a staccato effect that can make your writing sound like a
child's reader: "This is my dog. See him run."

Use contrast. Just as a jeweller will highlight a diamond by displaying it against dark velvet, so you can highlight an idea by placing it against a contrasting background:

orig. Most employees in industry do not have indexed pensions.

rev. Unlike civil servants, most employees in industry do not have indexed pensions.

Using parallel phrasing will increase the effect of the contrast:

> Although he often gave informal talks, he seldom gave presentations at conferences.

Use a well-placed adverb or correlative construction. Adding an adverb or two can sometimes help you to dramatize a concept:

orig. Although I dislike the proposal, I must accept it as the practical answer.

rev. Although emotionally I dislike the proposal, intellectually I must accept it as the practical answer.

Correlatives such as *both . . . and* or *not only . . . but also* can be used to emphasize combinations as well:

orig. Smith was a good teacher and a good friend.

rev. Smith was both a good teacher and a good friend.

rev. Smith was not only a good teacher but also a good friend.

Use your ears

Your ears are probably your best critics: make good use of them. Before producing a final copy of any piece of writing, read it out loud, in a clear voice. The difference between cumbersome and fluent passages will be unmistakable.

Some final advice: write before you revise

No one would expect you to sit down and put all this advice into practice as soon as you start to write. You would feel so constrained that it would be hard to get anything down on paper at all. You will be better off if you begin practising these techniques during the editing process, when you are looking critically at what you have already written. Some experienced writers can combine the creative and critical functions, but most of us find it easier to write a rough draft first, before starting the detailed task of revising.

REFERENCES

Cluett, R. & Ahlborn, L. (1965). *Effective English prose*. New York: L. W. Singer Co.

8
Writing
tests and
examinations

If you are like most students, you will have to write quite a few exams in the course of your university career. Exams come in all shapes and sizes. In the arts and humanities most take the form of essays, but in the sciences many are either multiple-choice or the kind that require true-or-false answers. In this chapter we will give some suggestions to help you cope with exams.

GENERAL GUIDELINES

Before the exam

No matter what type of examination you take, you need to be prepared. This does not mean sitting down a couple of nights before the exam and trying to read and remember everything in your textbook. It does not even mean reading passively through your notes and texts once a week throughout the term. Studying is an active process, and if you develop good study skills you will have a head start on doing well in whatever exams you take.

The strategy suggested here is based on one developed by the learning-skills counsellors at the University of Western Ontario. You may regard this as a model for exam preparation which you can adapt to fit your own needs. The most important thing to remember is to be organized and to use your time effectively.

There are six steps to consider in preparing for an exam:

GET A PERSPECTIVE
(Survey)
↓
LEARN THE MATERIAL
(Comprehension/Memory)
↓
CONSOLIDATE AND ANTICIPATE
(Prediction)
↓
SIMULATE THE TEST
(Testing)
↓
FILL IN THE GAPS
(Comprehension/Memory)
↓
FINAL REVIEW
(Checking)

1.Get a perspective

Bring together all the materials you have accumulated during the course—textbook, course outline, lecture notes, notes you have made yourself from the textbook, and so on. Skim through this material to regain a sense of what the course was about and what the main topic areas were. Even at this stage you should be able to identify general areas from which questions might be drawn.

2. Learn the material

This stage will be much easier if you have spent some time after each lecture reviewing the text and your notes. Weekly review of texts and lecture notes will help you not only to remember important material, but to relate new information to old. If you don't review regularly, at the end of the year you'll be faced with relearning rather than remembering.

Set memory triggers. As you review, condense and focus the material by writing down in the margin key words or phrases that will trigger off a whole set of details in your mind. The trigger might be a concept word that names or points to an important theory or definition,

or a quantitative phrase such as "three factors affecting the development of schizophrenia" or "four classes of operant conditioning."

Sometimes you can create an acronym or a nonsense sentence that
will trigger an otherwise hard-to-remember set of facts—something
like the mnemonic "Oh, Oh, Oh, To Touch And Feel A Green Vervet
At Home"—to remind you of the initial letters of the twelve cranial
nerves. Simply grouping related items can be a big help: it's much
easier to remember thirty facts as five sets of six each than as individual items. Because the difficulty of memorizing increases with the
number of individual items you are trying to remember, any method
that will reduce the number will increase your effectiveness.

Don't just memorize. At this stage it's a good idea to rewrite and
condense your notes so that you can go through them quickly during
your final review. At the same time, make very sure that you really
understand the material. Trying to learn by rote something you don't
understand is far more difficult than simply hanging facts on a well-
understood framework.

Whatever your study plan, do not simply read through your text
and other course materials without making notes, asking questions,
or solving problems. Something that seems quite straightforward when
you read it may turn out to be much less clear when you have to write
about it.

3. Consolidate and anticipate

Now you should start thinking specifically about what questions may
be on the exam. Analyse the main ideas and most important details
presented in the course, and then try to make up some questions based
on them. Even if the exam questions are phrased quite differently,
thinking about the course material in terms of questions should help
you to make the necessary connections when you are in the exam room.

In addition to making up your own questions, you should try to
look over some previous exam papers. Old examinations are useful
both for seeing the type of question you might be asked and for checking on the thoroughness of your preparation. If old exams aren't available, you might get together with friends taking the same course and
ask each other questions. Just remember that the most useful review
questions are not the ones that require you to recall facts, but those
that force you to analyse, integrate, or evaluate information.

4. Simulate the test

Set a hypothetical exam for yourself. This may be a combination of old exam questions and ones that you have made up yourself—it doesn't really matter. Then find a time when you will be free of interruptions and write the exam as if it were the real thing. Although this takes a lot of self-discipline, it is an excellent way to find out your strengths and weaknesses.

5. Fill in the gaps

After your reviews and self-testing you can start to go over those areas that need further study. Don't waste time on things you already know well; just fill in the gaps.

6. Final review

The day before the exam, go over your condensed notes and rehearse some possible questions. At this stage you should have done all of your work to understand and memorize the material. Now you need to get yourself into a frame of mind to take the exam.

Test anxiety

Most students feel nervous before examinations. It's not surprising. Writing an exam of any kind imposes strong pressures. In an essay exam, because the time is restricted, you can't edit and rewrite the way you can in a regular essay; because the questions are restricted, you must write on topics you might otherwise choose to avoid. If you are writing a multiple-choice exam, often you don't know whether you are interpreting the questions correctly—and if there is a penalty for guessing, you have the extra stress of deciding whether to take on an answer that you aren't sure is correct. You know that to do your best you need to feel calm—but how? It may be of some comfort to know that a moderate level of anxiety is beneficial: it keeps you alert. It's when you are overconfident or paralysed with fear that you run into difficulties.

There are many strategies for coping with test anxiety, but perhaps the best general advice is to try to control your stress in a positive way. For example, give yourself lots of time to get to the exam; don't worry about how other students might be performing; don't keep generating negative "what-if" possibilities. Even if you can't turn off your worries, you can reduce them to the point that you can perform well.

AT THE EXAM

If you look at the question paper and your first reaction is "I can't do any of it!", force yourself to keep calm; take ten slow, deep breaths as a deliberate relaxation exercise. Decide which is the question that you can answer best. Even if the exam seems disastrous at first, you can probably find one question that looks manageable: that's the one to begin with. It will get you rolling and increase your confidence. By the time you have finished, you are likely to find that your mind has worked through to the answer for another question.

Essay exams

Read the exam

An exam is not a hundred-metre dash; instead of starting to write immediately, take time at the beginning to read through each question and create a plan of action. A few minutes spent on thinking and organizing will bring better results than the same time spent writing a few more lines.

Apportion your time

Read the instructions carefully to find out how many questions you must answer and to see if you have any choice. Subtract five minutes or so for the initial planning, then divide the time you have left by the number of questions you have to answer. If possible, allow for a little extra time at the end to reread and edit your work. If the instructions on the exam indicate that not all questions are of equal value, apportion your time accordingly.

Choose your questions

Decide on the questions that you will do and the order in which you will do them. Your answers don't have to be in the same order as the questions. If you think you have lots of time, it's a good idea to place your best answer(s) first, your worst in the middle, and your second-best at the end, in order to leave the reader on a high note. If you think you will be rushed, though, it's wiser to work from best to worst. That way you will be sure to get all the marks you can on your good answers, and you won't have to cut a good answer short at the end.

Read each question carefully

As you turn to each question, read it again carefully and underline all the key words. The wording will probably suggest the number of parts your answer should have; be sure you don't overlook anything (a common mistake when people are nervous). Since the verb used in the question is usually a guide for the approach to take in your answer, it's especially important that you interpret the following terms correctly:

- *explain*: show how or why something happens;
- *compare*: give both similarities and differences—even if the question doesn't say *compare and contrast*;
- *outline*: state simply, without much development of each point (unless specifically asked);
- *discuss*: develop your points in an orderly way, taking into account contrary evidence or ideas.

Make notes

Before you even begin to organize your answer, jot down key ideas and information related to the topic on rough paper or the unlined pages of your answer book. These notes will save you the worry of forgetting something by the time you begin writing. Next, arrange those parts you want to use into a brief plan.

Be direct

Get to the major points quickly and illustrate them frequently. In an exam, as opposed to a term paper, it's best to use a direct approach. Don't worry about composing a graceful introduction: simply state the main points that you are going to discuss, and then get on with developing them. Remember that your paper will likely be one of many read and marked by someone who has to work quickly—the clearer your answers are, the better they will be received.

For each main point give the kind of specific details that will prove you really know the materials. General statements will show you are able to assimilate information, but they need examples to back them up.

Write legibly

Writing that is hard to read produces a cranky reader. When the marker has to struggle to decipher your ideas, you may get poorer results than you deserve. If for some special reason (such as a physical impairment) your writing is hard to read, see if you can make special arrangements to use a typewriter. If your writing is just plain bad, it's probably better to print.

Write on alternate lines

Writing on every other line will not only make your writing easier to read, but leave you space for changes and additions; you won't have to cover your paper with a lot of messy circles and arrows.

Keep to your time plan

Keep to your plan and don't skip any questions. Try to write something on each topic. Remember that it's easier to score half marks for a question you don't know much about than it is to score full marks for one you could write pages on. If you find yourself running out of time on an answer and still haven't finished, summarize the remaining points and go on to the next question. Leave a large space between questions so that you can go back and add more if you have time. If you write a new ending, remember to cross out the old one—neatly.

Reread your answers

No matter how tired or fed up you are, reread your answers at the end, if there's time. Check especially for clarity of expression; try to get rid of confusing sentences and increase the logical connection between your ideas. Revisions that make answers easier to read are always worth the effort.

Multiple-choice exams

Many students are terrified of multiple-choice exams. They're afraid that the questions will require minutely detailed knowledge of the subject material and that they may be ambiguous. In some cases this is true, but often the problem lies in the student's test-taking strategies. Richard Zajchowski, a learning-skills counsellor, has suggested that students adopt a conscious exam-writing procedure:

1. Read the question (not the answers) twice to get (a) concepts, and (b) context. (What is the question really asking? You may need to translate it into your own words.)

2. Recall the appropriate conceptual information and try to think of the correct answer.

3. Now (and only now) read each alternative carefully. Again, you may need to translate the answers into your own words. Choose the one that best answers the meaning of the question. With luck, this will agree with the answer that you had generated yourself.

4. If there is no penalty for guessing, be sure to answer all the questions. It's unlikely that all your choices will be random, so you have a chance here to gain some extra points.

5. When you go back to look over your paper after answering all the questions you can, don't change any answers unless you are very sure: "second guesses" are often wrong.

Make educated guesses

If you are unsure about a particular question, make your guess an educated one. James F. Shepherd (1979, 1981) has suggested a number of strategies for improving your guesswork. Here are a few:

- Forget about intuition, lucky numbers, or patterns of right answers (the idea that if the last two correct answers have been "A", the next one can't be). Many test-setters deliberately try to foil pattern-hunters.

- Start by weeding out any answers that are clearly wrong.

- Avoid any terms that you don't recognize. Some students are taken in by anything that looks like scientific terminology and may assume that such an answer must be a sophisticated version of the right one. They are usually wrong: the unfamiliar term may well be a red herring, especially if it is close in sound to the correct one.

- Avoid extremes. Most often the right answer lies in between. For example, suppose that the options are the numbers 800,000; 350,000; 275,000; and 15: the highest and lowest numbers are likely to be wrong.

- Choose the best available answer, even if it is not indisputably true.

- Choose the long answer over the short (it's more likely to contain the detail needed to make it right) and the particular statement over the general (generalizations are usually too sweeping to be true).

• Choose "all of the above" over individual answers. Test-setters know that students with a patchy knowledge of the course material will often fasten on the one fact they know. Only those with a thorough knowledge will recognize that all the answers listed are correct.

Open-book exams

If you think that permission to take your books into the exam room is an "Open Sesame" to success, be forewarned. You could fall into the trap of relying too heavily on them; you may spend so much time flipping through pages and looking things up that you won't have time to write good answers. The result may be worse than if you had been allowed no books at all.

If you want to do well, use your books only to check information and to look up specific, hard-to-remember details for a topic you already know a good deal about. For instance, if your subject is biochemistry you can look up chemical formulae; if it is statistics you can look up equations; if it is psychology you can look up specific terms or experimental details. In other words, use the books to make sure your answers are precise and well illustrated. Never use them to replace studying and careful exam preparation.

Take-home exams

The benefit of a take-home exam is that you have time to plan your answers and to consult your texts or other sources. The catch is that the time is usually less than it would be for an ordinary essay. Don't work yourself into a frenzy trying to respond with a polished research essay for each question. Keep in mind that you were given this assignment to test your overall command of the course: your reader is likely to be less concerned with your specialized research than with evidence that you have understood and assimilated the material.

The guidelines for a take-home exam are similar to those for a regular exam; the only difference is that you don't need to keep such a close eye on the clock:

1. Keep your introduction short and get to the point quickly.

2. Have a straightforward and obvious organizational pattern so that the reader can easily see your main ideas.
3. Use concrete examples often to back up your points.
4. Where possible, show the range of your knowledge of course material by referring to a number of different sources, rather than constantly using the same ones.
5. Try to show that you can analyse and evaluate material: that you can do more than simply repeat information.

REFERENCES

Shepherd, J.F. (1979). *College study skills*. Boston: Houghton Mifflin.

Shepherd, J.F. (1981). *RSVP: The Houghton Mifflin reading, study and vocabulary program*. Boston: Houghton Mifflin.

9
Common errors in grammar and usage

This chapter is not a comprehensive grammar lesson: it's simply a survey of those areas where students most often make mistakes. It will help you keep a look-out for weaknesses as you are editing your work. Once you get into the habit of checking, it won't be long before you are correcting potential problems as you write.

The grammatical terms used here are the most simple and familiar ones; if you need to review some of them, see the Glossary. For a thorough treatment of grammar or usage see Thompson and Martinet (1980).

Troubles with sentence unity

Sentence fragments

To be complete, a sentence must have both a subject and a verb in an independent clause; if it doesn't, it's a fragment. When you are writing informally there are times when a sentence fragment is acceptable to emphasize a point, as in:

> What is the probability of contracting tuberculosis through casual contact? Very low.

Here the sentence fragment *Very low* is clearly intended to be understood as a short form of *The probability is very low*. Unintentional sentence fragments, on the other hand, usually seem incomplete rather than shortened:

✗   The liquid was poured into a glass beaker. <u>Being a strong acid</u>.

The last "sentence" is incomplete because it has no subject or verb. (Remember that a participle such as *being* is a verbal, not a verb; in fact, any *-ing* word by itself is not a verb.) The sentence can be made complete by adding a subject and a verb:

✓   <u>The liquid was</u> a strong acid.

Alternatively, you could join the fragment to the preceding sentence:

✓   The liquid was poured into a glass beaker, because it was a strong acid.

✓   Because the liquid was a strong acid, it was poured into a glass beaker.

Run-on sentences

A run-on sentence is one that continues beyond the point where it should have stopped:

✗   The subjects who took part in the experiment all said they enjoyed participating, even though it lasted for two hours, and they all agreed to come back for a second session.

The *and* should be dropped and a period or semicolon added after *hours*.

Another kind of run-on sentence is one in which two independent clauses (phrases that could stand by themselves as sentences) are joined incorrectly by a comma:

✗   The instructions called for 50 g of sugar to be added, we used fructose in our experiment.

This error is known as a *comma splice*. There are three ways of correcting it:

- by putting a period after *added* and starting a new sentence:

✓   . . . to be added. We . . .

- by replacing the comma with a semicolon:

✓   . . . to be added; we . . .

- by making one of the independent clauses subordinate to the other:

✓   The instructions, which called for 50 g of sugar to be added, allowed us to use fructose in our experiment.

Contrary to what many people think, words such as *however, there-fore*, and *thus* cannot be used to join independent clauses:

✗   Two of my friends started out in science, however, they
quickly decided they didn't like chemistry.

The mistake can be corrected by beginning a new sentence after *science*
or (preferably) by putting a semicolon in the same place:

✓   Two of my friends started out in science; however, they
quickly decided they didn't like chemistry.

The only words that can be used to join independent clauses are
the coordinating conjunctions — *and, or, nor, but, for, yet,* and *so* —
and subordinating conjunctions such as *if, because, since, while, when,
where, after, before,* and *until*.

Faulty predication

When the subject of a sentence is not connected grammatically to
what follows (the predicate), the result is faulty predication:

✗   The <u>reason</u> he failed was <u>because</u> he couldn't handle multiple choice exams.

The problem is that *because* means essentially the same thing as *the
reason for*. The subject needs a noun clause to complete it:

✓   The <u>reason</u> he failed was <u>that</u> he couldn't handle multiple
choice exams.

Another solution would be to rephrase the sentence:

✓   He failed because he couldn't handle multiple choice exams.

Faulty *is when* or *is where* constructions can be corrected in the same
way:

✗   The difficulty <u>is when</u> the two sets of data disagree.

✓   The difficulty <u>arises when</u> the two sets of data disagree.

Troubles with subject-verb agreement

Identifying the subject

A verb should always agree in number with its subject. Sometimes,
however, when the subject does not come at the beginning of the sentence, or when it is separated from the verb by other information,

you may be tempted to use a verb form that does not agree:

✗　The change in the viscosity and the rate of flow <u>were mea-sured</u> by the investigators.

The subject here is *change*, not *viscosity and the rate of flow*; therefore the verb should be the singular *was measured*:

✓　The change in the viscosity and the rate of flow <u>was mea-sured</u> by the investigators.

Either, neither, each

The indefinite pronouns *either*, *neither*, and *each* always take singular verbs:

✗　<u>Neither</u> of the cats <u>have</u> a flea collar.

✓　<u>Each</u> of them <u>has</u> a rabies tag.

Compound subjects

When *or*, *either . . . or*, or *neither . . . nor* is used to create a compound subject, the verb should usually agree with the last item in the subject:

✓　Neither the professor nor his <u>students were able</u> to solve the equation.

If a singular item follows a plural item, however, a singular verb may sound awkward, and it's better to rephrase the sentence:

orig.　Either my history <u>books</u> or my biology <u>text is going</u> to gather dust this weekend.

rev.　This weekend, I'm going to leave behind either my history books or my biology text.

Unlike the word *and*, which creates a compound subject and therefore takes a plural verb, *as well as* or *in addition to* does not create a compound subject; therefore the verb remains singular:

✓　Organic chemistry <u>and</u> applied math <u>are</u> difficult subjects.

✓　Organic chemistry <u>as well as</u> applied math <u>is</u> a difficult subject.

Collective nouns

A collective noun is a singular noun, such as *family*, *army*, or *team*, that includes a number of members. If the noun refers to the members as a unit, it takes a singular verb:

✓   The <u>class goes</u> on a field trip in June.

If the noun refers to the members as individuals, however, the verb becomes plural:

✓   The <u>team are receiving</u> their prizes this week.

✓   The <u>majority</u> of bears <u>hibernate</u> in winter.

Titles

A title is singular even if it contains plural words; therefore it takes a singular verb:

✓   <u>Brain Mechanisms of Spatial Vision</u> is an interesting book.

✓   <u>Bausch and Lomb</u> is a company that makes microscopes.

Troubles with tense

Native speakers of English usually know the correct sequence of a verb tense by ear, but a few tenses can still be confusing.

The past perfect

If the main verb is in the past tense and you want to refer to something before that time, use the past perfect (*had* plus the past participle). The time sequence will not be clear if you use the simple past in both clauses:

✗   He hoped that she <u>bought</u> the computer.

✓   He hoped that she <u>had bought</u> the computer.

Similarly, when you are reporting what someone said in the past — that is, when you are using past indirect discourse — you should use the past perfect tense in the clause describing what was said:

✗   He said that the party <u>caused</u> the neighbours to complain.

✓   He said that the party <u>had caused</u> the neighbours to complain.

Using "if"

When you are describing a possibility in the future, use the present tense in the condition (*if*) clause and the future tense in the consequence clause:

✓   If he tests us on short-term memory, I <u>will fail</u>.

When the possibility is unlikely, it is conventional—especially in formal writing—to use the subjunctive in the *if* clause, and *would* plus the base verb in the consequence clause:

✓   If he <u>were to cancel</u> the test, I <u>would cheer</u>.

When you are describing a hypothetical instance in the past, use the past subjunctive (it has the same form as the past perfect) in the *if* clause and *would have* plus the past participle for the consequence. A common error is to use *would have* in both clauses:

✗   If he <u>would have been</u> more friendly, I <u>would have asked</u> him to be my lab partner.

✓   If he <u>had been</u> more friendly, I <u>would have asked</u> him to be my lab partner.

Troubles with pronouns

Pronoun reference

The link between a pronoun and the noun it refers to must be clear. If the noun doesn't appear in the same sentence as the pronoun, it should appear in the preceding sentence:

✗   The textbook supply in the bookstore had run out, so we borrowed <u>them</u> from the library.

Since *textbook* is used as an adjective rather than a noun, it cannot serve as a referent or antecedent for the pronoun *them*. You must either replace *them* or change the phrase *textbook supply*:

✓   The <u>textbook supply</u> in the bookstore had run out, so we borrowed <u>the texts</u> from the library.

✓   The textbooks in the bookstore had run out, so we borrowed them from the library.

When a sentence contains more than one noun, make sure there is no ambiguity about which noun the pronoun refers to:

✗   The faculty want <u>increased salaries</u> as well as <u>fewer teaching hours</u>, but the administration does not favour them.

What does the pronoun *them* refer to? The salary increases, the reduced teaching load, or both?

Using "it" and "this"

Using *it* and *this* without a clear referent can lead to confusion:

X Although the directors wanted to meet in January, it (this) didn't take place until May.

✓ Although the directors wanted to meet in January, the conference didn't take place until May.

Make sure that *it* or *this* clearly refers to a specific noun or pronoun.

Pronoun agreement

A pronoun should agree in number and person with the noun that it refers to:

X When a student is sick, their class-mates usually help out.

✓ When a student is sick, his class-mates usually help out.

Traditionally, the word *his* has been used to indicate both male and female, and most grammarians still maintain that *his* is the correct form. If you feel uncomfortable about using *his* alone, or want to avoid charges of sexism, now and again you may resort to the more cumbersome *his or her*, as this handbook occasionally does. Where possible, though, it's better to try switching from the singular to the plural in both noun and pronoun:

> When students are sick, their class-mates usually help out.

Using "one"

People often use the word *one* to avoid over-using *I* in their writing. Although in Britain this is common, in Canada and the United States frequent use of *one* may seem too formal and even a bit pompous:

✓ If one were to apply for the grant, one would find oneself engulfed in so many bureaucratic forms that one's patience would be stretched thin.

As a way out, it's becoming increasingly common in North America to use the third-person *his* or *her* as the adjectival form of *one* (this doesn't mean that you can substitute the nominative *he* or *she* for *one* as the subject):

> One would find his patience stretched thin.

In any case, try to use *one* sparingly, and don't be afraid of the occasional *I*. The one serious error to avoid is mixing the third-person *one* with the second-person *you*.

✗   When <u>one</u> visits the cyclotron, <u>you</u> are impressed by its size.

In formal academic writing generally, *you* is not an appropriate substitute for *one*.

Using "me" and other objective pronouns

Remembering that it's wrong to say "Jane and me were invited to the party," rather than "Jane and I were invited," many people use the subjective form of the pronoun even when it should be objective:

✗   He invited Jane and <u>I</u> to the party.

✓   He invited Jane and <u>me</u> to the party.

The verb *invited* requires an object; *me* is the objective case. The same problem often arises following a preposition:

✗   <u>Between</u> you and <u>I</u>, this result doesn't make sense.

✓   <u>Between</u> you and <u>me</u>, this result doesn't make sense.

✗   Eating well is a problem <u>for we</u> students.

✓   Eating well is a problem <u>for us</u> students.

There are times, however, when the correct case can sound stiff or awkward:

orig. To whom was the award given?

Rather than keeping to a correct but awkward form, try to reword the sentence:

rev. Who received the award?

Exceptions for pronouns following prepositions

The rule that a pronoun following a preposition takes the objective case has exceptions. When the preposition is followed by a clause, the pronoun should take the case required by its position in the clause:

✗   The Chairman showed some concern over <u>whom would be</u> <u>selected as Dean.</u>

Although the pronoun follows the preposition *over*, it is also the subject of the verb *would be selected* and therefore requires the subjective case:

✓ The Chairman showed some concern over <u>who would be selected</u> as Dean.

Similarly, when a gerund (a word that acts partly as a noun and partly as a verb) is the subject of a clause, the pronoun that modifies it takes the possessive case:

✗ We were surprised by <u>him dropping</u> out of school.

✓ We were surprised by <u>his dropping</u> out of school.

Troubles with modifying

Adjectives modify nouns; adverbs modify verbs, adjectives, and other adverbs. Do not use an adjective to modify a verb:

✗ He played <u>good</u>. (Adjective with verb)

✓ He played <u>well</u>. (Adverb modifying verb)

✓ He played <u>really well</u>. (Adverb modifying adverb)

✓ He had a <u>good style</u>. (Adjective modifying noun)

✓ He had a <u>really good style</u>. (Adverb modifying adjective)

Squinting modifiers

Remember that clarity depends very much on word order: to avoid confusion, the relations between the different parts of a sentence must be clear. Modifiers should therefore be as close as possible to the words they modify. A squinting modifier is one that, because of its position, seems to look in two directions at once:

✗ She discovered <u>in the spring</u> she was going to have to write her final exams.

Was spring the time of the discovery or the time of the exams? The logical relation is usually clearest when you place the modifier immediately in front of the element it modifies:

✓ <u>In the spring</u> she <u>discovered</u> that she was going to have to write her final exams.

✓ She discovered that she would have to write her <u>final exams in the spring</u>.

Other squinting modifiers can be corrected in the same way:

✗   Our biology professor gave a lecture on Planaria, which was well-illustrated.

✓   Our biology professor gave a well-illustrated lecture on Planaria.

Dangling modifiers

Modifiers that have no grammatical connection with anything else in the sentence are said to be dangling:

✗   Walking around the campus in June, the river and trees made a picturesque scene.

Who is doing the walking? Here's another example:

✗   Reflecting on the results of the study, it was decided not to submit the paper for publication.

Who is doing the reflecting? Clarify the meaning by connecting the dangling modifier to a new subject:

✓   Walking around the campus in June, she thought the river and trees made a picturesque scene.

✓   Reflecting on the results of the study, they decided not to submit the paper for publication.

Troubles with pairs (and more)

Comparisons

Make sure that your comparisons are complete. The second element in a comparison should be equivalent to the first, whether the equivalence is stated or merely implied:

✗   Today's students have a greater understanding of calculus than their parents.

The sentence suggests that the two things being compared are *calculus* and *parents*. Adding a second verb (*have*) equivalent to the first one shows that the two things being compared are *parents' understanding* and *students' understanding*:

✓   Today's students have a greater understanding of calculus than their parents have.

A similar problem arises in the following comparison:

X   The new text is a <u>boring book</u> and so are the lectures.

The lectures may be boring but they are not *a boring book*; to make sense, the two parts of the comparison must be parallel:

✓   The new text is <u>boring</u> and so are the lectures.

Correlatives (coordinate constructions)

Constructions such as *both . . . and, not only . . . but,* and *neither nor* are especially tricky. The coordinating term must not come too early, or else one of the parts that come after will not connect with the common element. For the implied comparison to work, the two parts that come after the coordinating term must be grammatically equivalent:

X   He <u>not only</u> studies music <u>but</u> math.

✓   He studies <u>not only</u> music <u>but</u> math.

Parallel phrasing

A series of items in a sentence should be phrased in parallel wording. Make sure that all the parts of a parallel construction are really equal:

X   We had to turn in <u>our</u> rough notes, <u>our</u> calculations, and finished assignment.

✓   We had to turn in <u>our</u> rough notes, <u>our</u> calculations, and <u>our</u> finished assignment.

Once you have decided to include the pronoun *our* in the first two elements, the third must have it too.

For clarity as well as stylistic grace, keep similar ideas in similar form:

X   He <u>failed</u> genetics and <u>barely passed</u> statistics, but zoology <u>was</u> a subject he did well in.

✓   He <u>failed</u> genetics and <u>barely passed</u> statistics, but <u>did well</u> in zoology.

REFERENCES

Thompson, A.J. & Martinet, A.V. (1980). *A practical English grammar* (3rd ed.). Oxford: Oxford University Press.

10
Punctuation

Punctuation causes students so many problems that it deserves a chapter of its own. If your punctuation is faulty, your readers will be confused and may have to backtrack; worse still, they may be tempted to skip over the rough spots. Punctuation marks are the traffic signals of writing; use them with precision to keep readers moving smoothly through your work.

PERIOD [.]

1. Use a period at the end of a sentence. A period indicates a full stop, not just a pause.

2. Use a period with abbreviations. British style omits the period in certain cases, but North American style usually requires it for abbreviated titles (Ms., Dr., etc.) as well as place-names (B.C., N.W.T., etc.). Although the abbreviations and acronyms for some organizations include periods, the most common ones generally do not (CIDA, CARE, etc.).

3. Use a period at the end of an indirect question. Do *not* use a question mark:

  ✗   He asked if I wanted a clean lab coat?

  ✓   He asked if I wanted a clean lab coat.

COMMA [,]

Commas are the trickiest of all punctuation marks; even the experts differ on when to use them. Most agree, however, that too many commas are as bad as too few, since they make writing choppy and awkward to read. Certainly, recent writers use fewer commas than earlier writers did. Whenever you are in doubt, let clarity be your guide. The most widely accepted conventions are these:

1. Use a comma to separate two independent clauses joined by a coordinating conjunction (*and, but, for, or, nor, yet, so*). By signalling that there are two clauses, the comma will prevent the reader from confusing the beginning of the second clause with the end of the first:

✗   He finished working with the microscope and his partner turned off the power.

✓   He finished working with the microscope, and his partner turned off the power.

When the second clause has the same subject as the first, you have the option of omitting both the second subject and the comma:

✓   He writes well, but he never finishes on time.

✓   He writes well but never finishes on time.

If you mistakenly punctuate two sentences as if they were one, the result will be a *run-on sentence*; if you use a comma but forget the coordinating conjunction, the result will be a *comma splice*:

✗   He took his class to the zoo, it was closed for repairs.

✓   He took his class to the zoo, but it was closed for repairs.

Remember that words such as *however, therefore*, and *thus* are *conjunctive adverbs*, not conjunctions: if you use one of them the way you would use a conjunction, the result will again be a *comma splice*:

✗   She was accepted into medical school, however, she took a year off to earn her tuition.

✓   She was accepted into medical school; however, she took a year off to earn her tuition.

Conjunctive adverbs are often confused with conjunctions. You can distinguish between the two if you remember that a conjunctive adverb's position in a sentence can be changed:

✓   She was accepted into medical school; she took a year off, <u>however</u>, to earn her tuition.

The position of a conjunction, on the other hand, is invariable; it must be placed between the two clauses:

✓ She was accepted into medical school, <u>but</u> she took a year off to earn her tuition.

When, in rare cases, the independent clauses are short and closely related, they may be joined by a comma alone:

✓ I came, I saw, I conquered.

A *fused sentence* is a run-on sentence in which independent clauses are slapped together with no punctuation at all:

✗ He watched the hockey game all afternoon the only exercise he got was going to the kitchen between periods.

A fused sentence sounds like breathless babbling—and it's a serious error.

2. Use a comma between items in a series. (Place a coordinating conjunction before the last item):

The suite where the animals were housed was large, bright, and clean.

It contained a cage-washer, a bottle-washer, and a place for storing the clean glassware.

The comma before the conjunction is optional:

We have an office, a lab and a surgery.

Sometimes, though, the final comma can help to prevent confusion:

We arranged to move the rats, the photographs of the lab, and the gerbil food.

In this case, the comma prevents the reader from thinking that *photographs* refers both to the *lab* and the *gerbil food*.

3. Use a comma to separate adjectives preceding a noun when they modify the same element:

It was a reliable, accurate weighing device.

When the adjectives do not modify the same element, however, you should not use a comma:

It was an expensive chemical balance.

Here *chemical* modifies *balance*, but *expensive* modifies the total phrase *chemical balance*. A good way of checking whether or not you need a comma is to see if you can reverse the order of the adjectives. If you can reverse it (*reliable, accurate balance* or *accurate, reliable balance*), use a comma; if you can't (*chemical expensive balance*), omit the comma.

4. Use commas to set off an interruption (an interrupting word or phrase is technically called a parenthetical element):

✓   The outcome, he said, was a complete failure.

✓   My tutor, however, couldn't answer the question.

Remember to put commas on both sides of the interruption:

✗   The equipment, they reported was obsolete.

✓   The equipment, they reported, was obsolete.

5. Use commas to set off words or phrases that provide additional but non-essential information:

> His grade on the test, the first of the year, was not very high.

> The new computer, his pride and joy, was always crashing.

The first of the year and *his pride and joy* are appositives: they give additional information about the nouns they refer to (*test* and *computer*), but the sentence would be understandable without them. Here's another example:

> Equinox magazine, which is published locally, often contains material that I can use in my course.

The phrase *which is published locally* is called a *non-restrictive modifier*, because it does not limit the meaning of the words it modifies (*Equinox magazine*). Without that modifying clause the sentence would still refer to the contents of the magazine. Since the information the clause provides is not necessary to the meaning of the sentence, you must use commas on both sides to set it off.

In contrast, a *restrictive* modifier is one that provides essential information; therefore it must not be set apart from the element it modifies, and commas should not be used:

> The issue that appeared last June was particularly useful.

Without the clause *that appeared last June* the reader would not know which issue was particularly useful.

To avoid confusion, be sure to distinguish carefully between essential and additional information. The difference can be important:

> Students who are not willing to work should not receive grants.
>
> Students, who are not willing to work, should not receive grants.

6. Use a comma after an introductory phrase when omitting it would cause confusion:

✗   In the room behind the professor's back, the students flew paper airplanes.

✓   In the room, behind the professor's back, the students flew paper airplanes.

7. Use a comma to separate elements in dates and addresses:

> February 2, 1986 (commas are often omitted if the day comes first: 2 February 1986)
>
> 117 Hudson Drive, Edmonton, Alberta.
>
> They lived in Dartmouth, Nova Scotia.

8. Use a comma before a quotation in a sentence:

> He stated, "E. coli was the bacterium isolated."
>
> "The most difficult part of the procedure," he reported, "was finding the material to work with."

For more formality, you may use a colon (see p. 99).

9. Use a comma with a name followed by a title:

> D. Gunn, Ph.D.
>
> Alice Smith, M.D.

SEMICOLON [;]

1. Use a semicolon to join independent clauses (complete sentences) that are closely related:

> For five days he worked non-stop; by Saturday he was exhausted.
>
> His lecture was confusing; no one could understand the terminology.

A semicolon is especially useful when the second independent clause begins with a conjunctive adverb such as *however, moreover, consequently, nevertheless, in addition*, or *therefore* (usually followed by a comma):

> He made several attempts; however, none of them was successful.

Some grammarians may disagree, but it's usually acceptable to follow a semicolon with a coordinating conjunction if the second clause is complicated by other commas:

> Some of these animals, wolverine and lynx in particular, are rarely seen; but occasionally, if you are patient, you might catch a glimpse of one.

2. Use a semicolon to mark the divisions in a complicated series when individual items themselves need commas. Using a comma to mark the subdivisions and a semicolon to mark the main divisions will help to prevent mix-ups:

> ✗ He invited Prof. Brooks, the vice-principal, Jane Hunter, and John Taylor.

Is the vice-principal a separate person?

> ✓ He invited Prof. Brooks, the vice-principal; Jane Hunter; and John Taylor.

In a case such as this, the elements separated by the semicolon need not be independent clauses.

COLON [:]

A colon indicates that something is to follow.

1. Use a colon before a formal statement or series:

> The layers are the following: sclera, choroid, and retina.

Do not use a colon if the words preceding it do not form a complete sentence:

> ✗ The layers are: sclera, choroid, and retina.
> ✓ The layers are sclera, choroid, and retina.

A colon is occasionally used, however, if the list is arranged vertically:

✓ The layers are: sclera,
                   choroid,
                   retina.

2. Use a colon for formality before a direct quotation:

> The leaders of the anti-nuclear group repeated their message: "The world needs bread before bombs."

DASH [—]

A dash creates an abrupt pause, emphasizing the words that follow. (Never use dashes as casual substitutes for other punctuation: overuse can detract from the calm, well-reasoned effect you want.)

1. Use a dash to stress a word or phrase:

> The fire alarm—which was deafening—warned them of the danger.

> I thought that writing this paper would be easy—when I started.

2. Use a dash in interrupted or unfinished dialogue:

> "It's a matter—to put it delicately—of personal hygiene."

In typing, use two hyphens together, with no spaces on either side, to show a dash.

EXCLAMATION MARK [!]

An exclamation mark helps to show emotion or feeling. It is usually found in dialogue:

> "Woe is me!" she mourned.

In scientific writing it is virtually never needed.

QUOTATION MARKS [" " or ' ']

Quotation marks are usually double in American style and single in British. In Canada either is accepted—just be consistent.

1. Use quotation marks to signify direct discourse (the actual words of a speaker):

> I asked, "What is the matter?"

He said, "I have a pain in my big toe."

2. Use quotation marks to show that words themselves are the issue:

The term "information processing" has a distinct meaning in psychology.

Alternatively, you may italicize or underline the terms in question.
Sometimes quotation marks are used to mark a slang word or an inappropriate usage, to show that the writer is aware of the difficulty:

Several of the "experts" did not seem to know anything about the topic.

Use this device only when necessary; usually it's better to let the context show your attitude, or to choose another term.

3. Use quotation marks to enclose quotations within quotations (single or double depending on your primary style):

She said, "Several of the 'experts' did not seem to know anything about the topic."

Placement of punctuation with quotation marks

Both the British and the American practices are accepted in Canada. British style usually places the punctuation outside the quotation marks, unless it is actually part of the quotation. The American practice, followed in this book, is increasingly common in Canada:

- A comma or period always goes inside the quotation marks:

He said, "Give me another chance," but I replied, "You've had enough chances."

- A semicolon or colon always goes outside the quotation marks:

George wants to watch "Second City"; I'd rather watch the hockey game.

- A question mark, dash, or exclamation mark goes inside quotation marks if it is part of the quotation, but outside if it is not:

He asked, "What's for dinner?"

Did he really call the boss a "lily-livered hypocrite"?

Her speech was hardly an appeal for "blood, sweat and tears"!

- When a reference is given parenthetically (in round brackets) at the end of a quotation, the quotation marks precede the parentheses and the sentence punctuation follows them:

  She said that "taking four aspirins a day reduces the risk of having a heart attack" (*The Medicine Show*, November 27, 1985).

APOSTROPHE [']

The apostrophe forms the possessive case for nouns and some pronouns.

1. Add an apostrophe followed by "s" to

- all singular and plural nouns not ending in *s*: *cat's, women's.*
- singular proper nouns ending in *s*: *Willis's, Collins's* (but note that the final *s* can be omitted if the word has a number of them already and would sound awkward, as in *Aloysius'*).
- indefinite pronouns: *someone's, anybody's,* etc.:

2. Add an apostrophe to plural nouns ending in "s": families', species', frogs'.

3. Do not add an apostrophe to set off an "s" when you are referring to numbers in the plural:

  These books were written in the 1920's.

  These books were written in the 1920s.

PARENTHESES [( )]

1. Use parentheses to enclose an explanation, example, or qualification. Parentheses show that the enclosed material is of incidental importance to the main idea. They make a less pronounced interruption than a dash, but a more pronounced one than a comma:

  The meerkat (a mongoose-like animal) is found in southern Africa.

  At least thirty people (according to the newspaper report) were under observation.

Remember that although punctuation should not precede parentheses, it may follow them if required by the sense of the sentence:

  I like coffee in the morning (if it's not instant), but she prefers tea.

If the parenthetical statement comes between two complete sentences, it should be punctuated as a sentence, with the period inside the
parentheses:

> I finished my last essay on April 3. (It was on long-term
> memory.) Fortunately, I had three weeks free to study for
> the exam.

2. **Use parentheses to enclose references.** See Chapter 5 for details.

BRACKETS [ ]

Brackets are square enclosures, not to be confused with parentheses
(which are round).

1. Use brackets to set off a remark of your own within a quotation.
They show that the words enclosed are not those of the person quoted:

> Mitchell stated, "Several of the changes observed [in the
> cat] are seen also in the monkey."

Brackets are sometimes used to enclose *sic* (Latin for *thus*), which
is used after an error, such as a misspelling, to show that the mistake
was in the original. *Sic* should be underlined:

> In describing the inhabitants of a tidal pool, he wrote that
> "it was almost impossible to loosen barnikles [sic] from
> the rock surface."

HYPHEN [-]

1. Use a hyphen if you must divide a word at the end of a line.
When a word is too long to fit at the end of a line, it's best to keep it in
one piece by starting a new line. But if you must divide, remember
these rules:

- Divide between syllables.
- Never divide a one-syllable word.
- Never leave one letter by itself.
- Divide double consonants except when they come before a suf-
  fix, in which case divide before the suffix:

> ar-rangement
> embar-rassment
> fall-ing
> pass-able

When the second consonant has been added to form the suffix, keep it with the suffix:

> refer-ral
> begin-ning

2. Use a hyphen to separate the parts of certain compound words:

> test-tube, vice-president (compound nouns)
>
> fine-tune, proof-read (compound verbs)
>
> well-designed study, sixteenth-century theory (compound adjectives used as modifiers preceding nouns).

When you are not using such expressions adjectivally, do not hyphenate them:

> The study was well designed.
>
> The theory was developed in the sixteenth century.

After long-time use, some compound nouns drop the hyphen. When in doubt, check a dictionary.

3. Use a hyphen with certain prefixes (*all-*, *self-*, *ex-*, and those prefixes preceding a proper name):

> all-trans retinal, self-imposed, ex-student, pro-nuclear

4. Use a hyphen to emphasize contrasting prefixes:

> The experiment required that we take both pre- and post-treatment measures.

5. Use a hyphen to separate written-out compound numbers from one to a hundred and compound fractions used as modifiers:

> eighty-one centimetres
>
> seven-tenths full

6. Use a hyphen to separate parts of inclusive numbers or dates:

> the years 1973-1976
> pages 3-40

ELLIPSIS [. . .]

1. Use an ellipsis to show an omission from a quotation:

> "The hormonal control of reproduction is modulated . . . ultimately by the production of gonadal steroids."

If the omission comes at the end of a sentence, the ellipsis is followed by a fourth period.

2. Use an ellipsis to show that a series of numbers continues indefinitely:

1,3,5,7,9 . . .

Catchlist of misused words and phrases

accept, except. Accept is a verb meaning to *receive affirmatively*; **except**, when used as a verb, means to *exclude*:

> I <u>accept</u> your offer.
> The teacher <u>excepted</u> him from the general punishment.

accompanied by, accompanied with. Use **accompanied by** for people; **accompanied with** for objects:

> He was <u>accompanied</u> by his wife.
> The brochure arrived, <u>accompanied with</u> a discount coupon.

advice, advise. Advice is a noun, **advise** a verb:

> He was <u>advised</u> to ignore the others' <u>advice</u>.

affect, effect. As a verb to **affect** means to *influence*; as a noun it's a technical psychological term. The verb to **effect** means to *bring about*. The noun means *result*. In most cases, you will be safe if you remember to use **affect** for the verb and **effect** for the noun:

> The eye drops <u>affect</u> her vision.
> The <u>effect</u> of the drops was to blur her vision.

all together, altogether. All together means *in a group*; **altogether** is an adverb meaning *entirely*:

> He was <u>altogether</u> certain that the books were <u>all together</u>.

alot. Write as two separate words: *a lot*.

allusion, illusion. An **allusion** is an indirect reference to something; an **illusion** is a false perception:

The comment about a caged animal was an <u>allusion</u> to his former supervisor.
He thought he saw a sea monster, but it was an <u>illusion</u>.

among, between. Use **among** for three or more persons or objects, **between** for two:

<u>Between</u> you and me, there's trouble <u>among</u> the team members.

amoral, immoral. **Amoral** means *non-moral* or outside the moral sphere; **immoral** means *wicked*:

As a bioethicist, he was <u>amoral</u> in his judgements.
Carrying out surgical procedures on unanaesthetized animals is <u>immoral</u>.

amount, number. Use **amount** for money or noncountable quantities; use **number** for countable items:

No <u>amount</u> of grant money or <u>number</u> of research assistants will make up for academic incompetence.

anyways. Non-standard English: use *anyway*.

as, because. **As** is a weaker conjunction than **because** and may be confused with *when*:

<u>As</u> I was working, I ate at my desk.
<u>Because</u> I was working, I ate at my desk.

He arrived <u>as</u> I was leaving.
He arrived <u>when</u> I was leaving.

as to. A common feature of bureaucratese; replace it with a single-word preposition such as *about* or *on*:

X They were concerned <u>as to</u> the range of disagreement.
✓ They were concerned <u>about</u> the range of disagreement.

X They recorded his comments <u>as to</u> the proposal.
✓ They recorded his comments <u>on</u> the proposal.

bad, badly. **Bad** is an adjective meaning *not good*:

The meat <u>tastes bad</u>.
He <u>felt bad</u> about forgetting the dinner party.

Badly is an adverb meaning *not well;* when used with the verbs **want** or **need**, it means *very much*:

We all agreed that he had conducted the interview <u>badly</u>.
I <u>badly</u> need a new lab coat.

beside, besides. Beside is a preposition meaning *next to*:

She worked <u>beside</u> her assistant.

Besides has two uses: as a preposition it means *in addition to*; as a conjunctive adverb it means *moreover*:

<u>Besides</u> recommending the changes, the consultants are implementing them.
<u>Besides,</u> it was hot and we wanted to rest.

between. See **among**.

bring, take. One **brings** something to a closer place and **takes** it to a farther one.

can, may. Can means to *be able*; **may** means to *have permission*:

<u>Can</u> you fix the lock?
<u>May</u> I have the key to the closet?

In speech, **can** is used to cover both meanings: in formal writing, however, you should observe the distinction.

can't hardly. A faulty combination of the phrases **can't** and **can hardly**. Use one or the other of them instead:

He <u>can't</u> write.
He <u>can hardly</u> write.

capital, capitol. As a noun **capital** may refer to a seat of government, the top of a pillar, an upper-case letter, or accumulated wealth. **Capitol** refers only to a specific American—or ancient Roman—legislative building.

complement, compliment. The verb to **complement** means to *complete*; to **compliment** means to *praise*:

His engineering skill <u>complements</u> the skills of the designers.
I <u>complimented</u> her on her outstanding report.

continual, continuous. Continual means *repeated over a period of time*; **continuous** means *constant* or *without interruption*:

The breakdowns caused <u>continual</u> delays in completing the project.
The solution must be stirred <u>continuously</u> for three hours.

could of. Incorrect, as are **might of, should of,** and **would of.** Replace **of** with *have*:

   ✗ He <u>could of</u> done it.
   ✓ He <u>could have</u> done it.
   ✓ They <u>might have</u> been there.
   ✓ I <u>should have</u> known.
   ✓ We <u>would have</u> left earlier.

council, counsel. Council is a noun meaning an *advisory* or *deliberative assembly*. **Counsel** as a noun means *advice* or *lawyer*; as a verb it means to *give advice*:

   The college <u>council</u> meets on Tuesday.
   We respect her <u>counsel</u>, because she's seldom wrong.
   As a camp <u>counsellor</u>, you may need to counsel parents as well as children.

criterion, criteria. A **criterion** is a standard for judging something. **Criteria** is the plural of **criterion** and thus requires a plural verb:

   These are my <u>criteria</u> for selecting the applicants.

data. The plural of *datum*, **data** is increasingly treated as a singular noun, but this usage is not yet acceptable in formal prose: use a plural verb.

different than. Incorrect. Use either **different from** (American usage) or **different to** (British).

disinterested, uninterested. Disinterested implies impartiality or neutrality; **uninterested** implies a lack of interest:

   As a <u>disinterested</u> observer, he was in a good position to judge the issue fairly.
   <u>Uninterested</u> in the proceedings, he yawned repeatedly.

due to. Although increasingly used to mean *because of*, **due** is an adjective and therefore needs to modify something:

   ✗ <u>Due</u> to his impatience, we lost the contract. [<u>Due</u> is dangling]
   ✓ The loss was <u>due to</u> his impatience.

farther, further. Farther refers to distance, **further** to extent:

   He paddled <u>farther</u> than his friends.
   He explained the plan <u>further</u>.

good, well. Good is an adjective, not an adverb. **Well** can be both: as an adverb, it means *effectively*; as an adjective, it means *healthy*:

> The growing conditions are <u>good</u>.
> She is a <u>good</u> histologist.
> She sections the tissue <u>well</u>.
> At last, he is <u>well</u> again after his long bout of flu.

hanged, hung. Hanged means *executed by hanging*. **Hung** means *suspended* or *clung to*:

> He was <u>hanged</u> at dawn for the murder.
> He <u>hung</u> the picture.
> He <u>hung</u> to the boat when it capsized.

hopefully. Use **hopefully** as an adverb meaning *full of hope*:

> She scanned the horizon <u>hopefully</u>, waiting for her friend's ship to appear.

In formal writing, using **hopefully** to mean *I hope* is still frowned upon, although increasingly common; it's better to use *I hope*:

> ✗ <u>Hopefully</u> we'll write more papers this year.
> ✓ <u>I hope</u> we'll write more papers this year.

imply, infer. Imply refers to what a statement suggests; **infer** relates to the audience's interpretation:

> His answer <u>implied</u> that he didn't really know.
> I <u>inferred</u> from his answer that he didn't really know.

irregardless. Redundant; use *regardless*.

its, it's. Its is a form of possessive pronoun; **it's** is a contraction of *it is*. Many people mistakenly put an apostrophe in **its** in order to show possession:

> ✗ The cub wanted <u>it's</u> mother.
> ✓ The cub wanted <u>its</u> mother.
> ✓ <u>It's</u> time to leave.

less, fewer. Use **less** for money and things that are not countable; use **fewer** for things that are:

> Now that he's earning <u>less</u> money he's going to <u>fewer</u> movies.

lie, lay. To **lie** means to *assume a horizontal position*; to **lay** means to *put down*. The changes of tense often cause confusion:

Present	Past	Past participle
lie	lay	lain
lay	laid	laid

like, as. Like is a preposition, but it is often wrongly used as a conjunction. To join two independent clauses, use the conjunction **as**:

  ✗ I want to progress <u>like</u> you have this year.
  ✓ I want to progress <u>as</u> you have this year.

  ✓ Prof. Dodd is <u>like</u> my old school principal.

might of. See **could of.**

myself, me. Myself is an intensifier of, not a substitute for, *I* or *me*:

  ✗ He gave it to John and <u>myself</u>.
  ✓ He gave it to John and <u>me</u>.

  ✗ Jane and <u>myself</u> are invited.
  ✓ Jane and <u>I</u> are invited.

  ✓ <u>Myself</u>, I would prefer a swivel chair.

nor, or. Use **nor** with **neither** and **or** by itself or with **either**:

  He is <u>neither</u> overworked <u>nor</u> underfed.
  The plant is <u>either</u> diseased <u>or</u> dried out.

off of. Remove the unnecessary **of**:

  ✗ The fence kept the children <u>off of</u> the premises.
  ✓ The fence kept the children <u>off</u> the premises.

phenomenon. A singular noun: the plural is **phenomena.**

principal, principle. As an adjective, **principal** means *main* or *most important*; a **principal** is the head of a school. A **principle** is a *law* or *controlling idea*:

  Our <u>principal</u> aim is to reduce the deficit.
  Our <u>principal</u>, Prof. Smart, retires next year.
  We are defending the island as a matter of <u>principle</u>.

rational, rationale. Rational is an adjective meaning *logical* or *able to reason*. **Rationale** is a noun meaning *explanation*:

  That was not a <u>rational</u> decision.
  The president sent around a memo with a <u>rationale</u> for his proposal.

real, really. The adjective **real** should never be used as an adverb; use *really* instead:

✓ We had <u>real</u> maple syrup with our pancakes.

✗ It was <u>real</u> good.
✓ It was <u>really</u> good.

set, sit. To **sit** means to *rest on the buttocks*; to **set** means to *put* or *place*:

After standing so long, you'll want to <u>sit</u> down.
Please <u>set</u> the bowl on the table.

should of. See **could of.**

their, there. **Their** is the possessive form of the third person plural pronoun. **There** is usually an adverb, meaning *at that place* or *at that point*; sometimes it is used as an expletive (an introductory word in a sentence):

They parked <u>their</u> bikes <u>there</u>.
<u>There</u> is no point in arguing with you.

to, too, two. **To** is a preposition, as well as part of the infinitive form of a verb:

We went <u>to town</u> in order <u>to shop</u>.

Too is an adjective showing degree (the soup is *too* hot) or an adverb meaning *moreover*. **Two** is the spelled version of the number 2.

while. To avoid misreadings, use **while** only when you mean *at the same time that*. Do not use it as a substitute for *although*, *whereas*, or *but*:

✗ <u>While</u> he's getting fair marks, he'd like to do better.
✗ I headed for home, <u>while</u> she decided to stay.
✓ He fell asleep <u>while</u> he was reading.

-wise. Never use **-wise** as a suffix to form new words when you mean *with regard to*:

✗ <u>Marks-wise</u> she did better than last year.
✓ <u>With regard to her marks</u>, she did better than last year.
(or) ✓ <u>Her marks</u> were better than last year.

your, you're. **Your** is a pronominal adjective used to show possession; **you're** is a contraction of *you are*:

<u>You're</u> likely to miss <u>your</u> train.

Glossary

abstract
a summary accompanying a formal scientific report or paper, briefly outlining the contents.

abstract language
theoretical language removed from concrete particulars: e.g., *justice, goodness, truth* (cf. **concrete language**).

acronym
a word made up of the first letters of a group of words: e.g., *NATO* for *North Atlantic Treaty Organization*.

active voice
see **voice**.

adjective
a word that modifies or describes a noun or pronoun, hence a kind of noun marker: e.g., *red, beautiful, solemn*. An **adjectival phrase** or **adjectival clause** is a group of words modifying a noun or pronoun.

adverb
a word that modifies or qualifies a verb, adjective, or adverb, often answering a question such as *how? why? when?* or *where?*: e.g., *slowly, fortunately, early, abroad*. An **adverbial phrase** or **adverbial clause** is a group of words modifying a verb, adjective, or adverb: e.g., *by force, in revenge*. See also **conjunctive adverb**.

agreement
consistency in tense, number, or person between related parts of a sentence: e.g., between subject and verb, or noun and related pronoun.

ambiguity
vague or equivocal language; meaning that can be taken two ways.

antecedent (referent)
the noun for which a pronoun stands.

appositive
a word or phrase that identifies a preceding noun or pronoun: e.g., *Mrs. Jones,* **my aunt,** *is sick*. The second phrase is said to be *in apposition* to the first.

article
a word that precedes a noun and shows whether the noun is definite or indefinite; a kind of determiner or noun-marker. **Indefinite article:** *a (an)*. **Definite article**: *the*.

assertion
a positive statement or claim: e.g., *The Senate is irrelevant*.

auxiliary
a verb used in combination with another verb to create a verb phrase; a helping verb used to create certain tenses and emphases: e.g., *could, do, may, will, have*.

bibliography

(a) a list of works referred to or found useful in the preparation of an essay or report; **(b)** a reference book listing works available in a particular subject.

case

the inflected form of pronouns (see **inflection**). **Subjective case**: *I, we, he, she, it, they*. **Objective case**: *me, us, him, her, it, them*. **Possessive case**: *my, our, his, her, its, their*.

circumlocution

a roundabout or circuitous expression: e.g., *in a family way* for *pregnant*; *at this point in time* for *now*.

clause

a group of words containing a subject and predicate. An **independent clause** can stand by itself as a complete sentence: e.g., *I bought a hamburger*. A **subordinate** or **dependent clause** cannot stand by itself but must be connected to another clause: e.g., **Since I was hungry**, *I bought a hamburger*.

cliché

a trite or well-worn expression that has lost its impact through overuse: e.g., *slept like a log, sunny disposition, tried and true*.

collective noun

a noun that is singular in form but refers to a group: e.g., *family, team, jury*. It may take either a singular or a plural verb, depending on whether it refers to individual members or to the group as a whole.

comma splice

see **run-on sentence**.

complement

a completing word or phrase that usually follows a linking verb to form a **subjective** complement: e.g., (1) *He is* **my father**. (2) *That cigar smells* **terrible**. If the complement is an adjective it is sometimes called a **predicate adjective**. An **objective complement** completes the direct object rather than the subject: e.g., *We found him* **honest and trustworthy**.

complex sentence

a sentence containing a dependent clause as well as an independent one: e.g., *I bought the ring, although it was expensive*.

compound sentence

a sentence containing two or more independent clauses: e.g., *I saw the car wreck and I reported it*. A sentence is called **compound-complex** if it contains a dependent clause as well as two independent ones: e.g., *When the fog lifted, I saw the car wreck and I reported it*.

conclusion

the part of an essay in which the findings are pulled together or implications revealed so that the reader has a sense of closure or completion.

concrete language

specific language, giving particular details (often details of sense): e.g., *red, corduroy dress, three long-stemmed roses* (cf. **abstract language**).

conjunction

an uninflected word used to link words, phrases, or clauses. A **coordinating conjunction** (e.g., *and, or, but, for, yet*) links two equal parts of a sentence. A **subordinating conjunction**, placed at the beginning of a subordinate clause, shows the logical dependence of that clause on another: e.g., (1) **Although** *I am poor, I am happy.* (2) **While** *others slept, he studied.* **Correlative conjunctions** are pairs of coordinating conjunctions (see **correlatives**).

conjunctive adverb

a type of adverb that shows the logical relation between the phrase or clause that it modifies and a preceding one: e.g., (1) *I sent the letter; it never arrived,* **however**. (2) *The battery died;* **therefore** *the car wouldn't start.*

connotation

associative meaning; the range of suggestion called up by a certain word. Apparent synonyms, such as *poor* and *underprivileged*, may have different connotations (cf. **denotation**).

context

the text surrounding a particular passage that helps to establish its meaning.

contraction

a word formed by combining and shortening two words: e.g., *isn't, can't, we're.*

coordinate construction

see **correlatives**.

copula verb

see **linking verb**.

correlatives (coordinates)

pairs of coordinating conjunctions: e.g., *either/or, neither/nor, not only/but.*

dangling modifier

a modifying word or phrase (often a participial phrase) that is not grammatically connected to any part of the sentence: e.g., **Walking to school**, *the street was slippery.*

demonstrative pronoun

a pronoun that points out something: e.g., (1) **This** *is his reason.* (2) **That** *looks like my lost earring.* When used to modify a noun or pronoun, a demonstrative pronoun becomes a kind of **pronominal adjective**: e.g., *this hat, those people.*

denotation

the literal or dictionary meaning of a word (cf. **connotation**).

diction

the choice of words with regard to their tone, degree of formality, or register. Formal diction is the language of orations and serious essays. The informal diction of everyday speech or conversational writing can, at its extreme, become slang.

discourse

talk, either oral or written. **Direct discourse** gives the actual words spoken or written: e.g., *Donne said,* **"No man is an island."** In writing, direct discourse is put in quotation marks.

Indirect discourse gives the meaning of the speech rather than the actual words. In writing, indirect discourse is not put in quotation marks: e.g., *He said that no one exists in an island of isolation.*

ellipsis marks
three spaced periods indicating an omission from a quoted passage.

endnote
a footnote or citation placed at the end of an essay or report.

essay
a literary composition on any subject. Some essays are descriptive or narrative, but in an academic setting most are expository (explanatory) or argumentative.

expletive
a grammatically meaningless exclamation or phrase. The most common expletives are the sentence beginnings *It is* and *There is (are).*

exploratory writing
the informal writing done to help generate ideas before formal planning begins.

footnote
a citation placed at the bottom of a page or the end of the composition (cf. **endnote**).

fused sentence
see **run-on sentence**.

general language
language lacking specific details; abstract language.

gerund
a verbal (part-verb) that functions as a noun and is marked by an *-ing* ending: e.g., **Swimming** *can help you become fit.*

grammar
a study of the forms and relations of words, and of the rules governing their use in speech and writing.

hypothesis
a supposition or trial proposition made as a starting point for further investigation.

hypothetical instance
a supposed occurrence; often shown by a clause beginning with *if.*

indefinite article
see **article**.

independent clause
see **clause**.

indirect discourse
see **discourse**.

infinitive
a type of verbal not connected to any subject: e.g., *to ask.* The **base infinitive** omits the *to*: e.g., *ask.*

inflection
the change in the form of a word to indicate number, person, case, tense, or degree.

integrate
combine or blend together.

intensifier (qualifier)
a word that modifies and adds emphasis to another word or phrase: e.g.,**very** *tired,* **quite** *happy,* *I* **myself**.

interjection
a remark or exclamation interposed
or thrown into a speech, usually
accompanied by an exclamation
mark: e.g., *Oh dear! Alas!*

interrogative sentence
a sentence that asks a question:
e.g., *What is the time?*

intransitive verb
a verb that does not take a direct
object: e.g., *fall, sleep, talk.*

italics
slanting type used for emphasis,
replaced in typescript by underlining.

jargon
technical terms used unnecessarily
or in inappropriate places: e.g.,
peer-group interaction for *friendship.*

linking verb (copula verb)
the verb *to be* used to join subject
to complement: e.g., *The apples
were ripe.*

literal meaning
the primary, or denotative,
meaning of a word.

logical indicator
a word or phrase—usually a
conjunction or conjunctive
adverb— that shows the logical
relation between sentences or
clauses: e.g., *since, furthermore,
therefore.*

misplaced modifier
a word or group of words that
causes confusion or misreading
because it is not placed next to
the element it should modify:
e.g., *I only ate the pie.* [Revised: *I
ate only the pie.*]

modifier
a word or group of words that
describes or limits another
element in the sentence.

mood
(a) as a grammatical term, the
form that shows a verb's function
(indicative, imperative, interrogative, or subjunctive);
(b) when applied to literature
generally, the state of mind or
feeling shown.

non-restrictive modifier
see **restrictive modifier**.

noun
an inflected part of speech
marking a person, place, thing,
idea, action, or feeling, and
usually serving as subject, object,
or complement. A **common
noun** is a general term: e.g., *dog,
paper, automobile.* A **proper noun**
is a specific name: e.g., *Mary,
Sudbury, Skidoo.*

object
(a) a noun or pronoun that, when
it completes the action of a verb,
is called a **direct object**: e.g.,
He passed the **puck**. An **indirect
object** is the person or thing
receiving the direct object: e.g.,
He passed the **puck** (direct object)
to **Richard** (indirect object).
(b) The noun or pronoun in a
group of words beginning with a
preposition; pronouns take the
objective case: e.g., *at the* house,
about **her**, *for* **me**.

objective complement
see **complement**.

objectivity
a disinterested stance; a position
taken without personal bias or
prejudice (cf. **subjectivity**).

outline
with regard to an essay or report, a brief sketch of the main parts; a written plan.

paragraph
a unit of sentences arranged logically to explain or describe an idea, event, or object; usually marked by indentation of the first line.

parallel wording
wording in which a series of items has a similar grammatical form: e.g., *At her marriage my grandmother promised* **to love, to honour, and to obey** *her husband.*

paraphrase
restate in different words.

parentheses
curved lines, enclosing and setting off a passage; not to be confused with square brackets.

parenthetical element
an interrupting word or phrase: e.g., *My musical career,* **if it can be called that**, *consisted of playing the triangle in kindergarten.*

participle
a verbal (part-verb) that functions as an adjective. Participles can be either **present**, usually marked by an -*ing* ending (e.g., *taking*), or **past** (*having taken*); they can also be passive (*having been taken*).

parts of speech
the major classes of words. Some grammarians include only function words (nouns, verbs, adjectives, and adverbs); others also include pronouns, prepositions, conjunctions, and interjections.

passive voice
see **voice**.

past participle
see **participle**.

periodic sentence
a sentence in which the normal order is inverted or an essential element suspended until the very end: e.g., *Out of the house, past the grocery store, through the school yard and down the railroad tracks* **raced the frightened boy**.

person
in grammar, the three classes of personal pronouns referring to the person speaking (first person), person spoken to (second person), and person spoken about (third person). With verbs, only the third person singular has a distinctive form.

personal pronoun
see **pronoun**.

phrase
a unit of words lacking a subject-predicate combination. The most common kind is the **prepositional phrase**—a unit comprising preposition plus object. Some modern grammarians also refer to the **single-word phrase**.

plural
indicating two or more in number. Nouns, pronouns, and verbs all have plural forms.

possessive case
see **case**.

prefix
a syllable placed in front of the root form of a word to make a new word: e.g., *pro-, in-, sub-* (cf. **suffix**).

preposition

a short word heading a unit of words containing an object, thus forming a **prepositional phrase**: e.g., **under** *the tree*, **before** *my time*.

pronoun

a word that stands in for a noun.

punctuation

a conventional system of signs used to indicate stops or divisions in a sentence and to make meaning clearer: e.g., comma, period, semicolon, etc.

reference works

material consulted when preparing an essay or report.

referent (antecedent)

the noun for which a pronoun stands.

relative clause

a clause headed by a relative pronoun: e.g., *the man* **who came to dinner** *is my uncle.*

relative pronoun

who, which, what, that, or their compounds beginning an adjective or noun clause: e.g., *the house* **that** *Jack built*; **whatever** *you say.*

restrictive element

a phrase or clause that identifies or is essential to the meaning of a term: e.g., *The book* **that I need** *is lost.* It should not be set off by commas. A non-restrictive element is not needed to identify the term and is usually set off by commas: e.g., *This book,* **which I got from my aunt**, *is one of my favourites.*

register

the degree of formality in word choice and sentence structure.

run-on sentence

a sentence that goes on beyond the point where it should have stopped. The term covers both the **comma splice** (two sentences joined by a comma) and the **fused sentence** (two sentences joined without any punctuation between them).

sentence

a grammatical unit that includes both a subject and a predicate. The end of a sentence is marked by a period.

sentence fragment

a group of words lacking either a subject or a verb; an incomplete sentence.

simple sentence

a sentence made up of only one clause: e.g., *Joan climbed the tree.*

slang

colloquial speech, not considered part of standard English; often used in a special sense by a particular group: e.g., *gross* for *disgusting*; *gig* as a musician's term.

split infinitive

a construction in which a word is placed between *to* and the base verb: e.g., *to completely finish.*

squinting modifier

a kind of misplaced modifier; one that could be connected to elements on either side, making meaning ambiguous: e.g., *When he wrote the letter* **finally** *his boss thanked him.*

standard English

the English currently spoken or written by literate people over a wide geographical area.

subject
in grammar, the noun or noun equivalent about which something is predicated; that part of a clause with which the verb agrees: e.g., **They** *swim every day when the* **pool** *is open.*

subjectivity
a personal stance, not impartial (cf. **objectivity**).

subjunctive
see **mood**.

subordinate clause
see **clause**.

subordinating conjunction
see **conjunction**.

subordination
making one clause in a sentence dependent on another.

suffix
an addition placed at the end of a word to form a derivative: e.g., *prepare—prepara***tion**; *sing—sing***ing** (cf. **prefix**).

synonym
a word with the same dictionary meaning as another word: e.g., *begin* and *commence*.

syntax
sentence construction; the grammatical relations of words.

tense
the time reference of verbs.

thesis statement
a one-sentence assertion that gives the central argument of an essay or thesis.

topic sentence
the sentence in a paragraph that expresses the main or controlling idea.

theme
a recurring or dominant idea.

transition word
a word that shows the logical relation between sentences or parts of a sentence and thus helps to signal the change from one idea to another: e.g., *therefore, also, accordingly.*

transitive verb
one that takes an object: e.g., *hit, bring, cover.*

usage
accepted practice.

verb
that part of a predicate expressing an action, state of being, or condition, telling what a subject is or does. Verbs inflect to show tense (time). The principal parts of a verb are the three basic forms from which all tenses are made: the base infinitive, the past tense, and the past participle.

verbal
a word that is similar in form to a verb but does not function as one: a participle, a gerund, or an infinitive.

voice
the form of a verb that shows whether the subject acted (active voice) or was acted upon (passive voice): e.g., *He* **hit** *the ball* (active). *The ball* **was hit** *by him* (passive). Only transitive verbs (verbs taking objects) can be passive.

Index